La Rochefoucauld

La Rochefoucauld

The Art of Abstraction

PHILIP E. LEWIS

Cornell University Press

ITHACA AND LONDON

Cornell University Press gratefully acknowledges a grant from the Andrew W. Mellon Foundation that aided in bringing this book to publication.

First published 1977 by Cornell University Press.
Published in the United Kingdom by Cornell University Press Ltd., 2–4 Brook Street, London W1Y 1AA.

International Standard Book Number 0–8014–0848–2
Library of Congress Catalog Card Number 76–28016
Printed in the United States of America by York Composition Co., Inc.
Librarians: Library of Congress cataloging information appears on the last page of the book.

Contents

Contents

Preface

During the past quarter-century, La Rochefoucauld has received much serious, often favorable attention from numerous
highly intelligent scholars (among others, Antoine Adam, Roland
Barthes, Paul Bénichou, W. G. Moore, Corrado Rosso, Jean
Starobinski). As a result, his stature in French literary and
intellectual history appears to be increasing. At the same time,
La Rochefoucauld's position as a classical "moralist" has re-
mained enigmatic and controversial; his work is commonly
viewed as a corpus of discontinuous assertions, more readily
identifiable in terms of its rigorous, acerbic tone than of a
"message" or ethical perspective, and more appropriate to the
occasional search for incisive, provocative insights than to careful, systematic study. A survey of the criticism devoted to La
Rochefoucauld might well begin with the telling observation that
he has been the subject of many brilliant articles but of almost no
worthwhile books. While the explanation of this phenomenon is
no doubt complex, the relative paucity of books clearly reflects
an important characteristic of the moralist's writing: its resistance
to a thoroughgoing, synthetic reading and interpretation. It is
in response to the intellectual challenge of this resistance that the
present study has been conceived.

A certain number of critical choices should be made explicit.
First, I have taken seriously the fairly standard assumption that

the achievement of significant understanding in criticism is a cumulative process, always drawing upon what has been discovered, conjectured, or mistaken before, necessarily relying far more on strategic repetition, careful correction, and intelligent synthesis than upon genuinely original insight. This book takes into account openly and at times *in extenso* those past readings of La Rochefoucauld that inevitably orient and enrich present interpretation.

Second, although in teaching classical French literature I have found it profitable to read La Rochefoucauld in conjunction with Descartes, Pascal, La Fontaine, and La Bruyère (among others), in this study I have tried to uphold an initial commitment to a fundamentally immanent approach to La Rochefoucauld's texts. It would be an oversimplification to attribute this confining critical posture solely to the easily recognizable influence of phenomenologically oriented criticism, devoted to the perception of the work of a writer in its (his) own terms. When I began working on the text of the *Maximes* several years ago, I was also closely attuned to the prospering structuralist movement and much interested in the project of a scientific formalism that structuralist critics were articulating. This viewpoint reinforced my sense, developed in reading the "literary history" of La Rochefoucauld, that his cryptic corpus, so immediately open to multifarious comparisons, should be examined with rigorous, uncompromising attention to its own self-sufficient literary and axiological integrity. Whence the minimal concern here with many problems of influence and possibilities for *rapprochement*, the interest and importance of which are not in question, and about which I expect to write in the future.

Finally, as the foregoing remarks suggest, the writing of this book was propelled, so to speak, by the confrontation between thematic and formalist criticism. From the outset, I sought to develop, exploit, and appreciate this opposition, but not necessarily to overcome it through a transcendental synthesis. The resulting argumentative pattern has something of a circular con-

figuration. Once the opposition is established, the analysis—
while attempting to respect certain basic formal characteristics of
the work—moves into a predominantly thematic vein and pursues an interpretation of La Rochefoucauld's position as a
moralist. Then, when the position thus formulated is considered
in the light of the work's epistemological perspective, the problem of form and its relation to meaning is regenerated and
treated explicitly, both as a problem of description and, at the
inevitable intersection of style with theme, as a problem of
interpretation.

The critical perspective within which the form/theme opposition is a major factor is an evanescent one. In 1976, five years
after the central part of my concluding chapter was composed, I
am acutely aware of the disrepute into which "conceptualist
thematicism" has fallen. The advent of "poststructuralist" theses
in philosophy, the remarkable development of discourse analysis
and, more generally, of a linguistics of performance, the elaboration of a problematics of textuality, and the burgeoning research
in the field of semiotics have begun to steer critical inquiry toward a theoretical horizon in which the processes of language
and writing can no longer be conceptualized in terms of forms
and themes and their tensions or connections. Yet I have chosen
not to disown the readings in which this study is anchored, for
the critical itinerary that I pursued in writing it seems to me to
have some exemplary value. As my book advances, the schematic
movement from the form/theme opposition through thematic
and formalist analyses back to their intersection is not represented as a closed critical circle, denying priority to either
thematics or formalism. On the contrary, the *closing* venture into
textual analysis, devoted to the nature of abstract discourse,
unmistakably grants the logical priority of lingual over conceptual determinations, and in so doing, implicitly views thematic
coherence as a by-product in the articulation of abstract discourse.
To be sure, the vein of discourse analysis is a deep and pervasive
one of which the present study has barely scratched the surface.

Insofar as the concluding chapter lies beyond the immediate
purview of both thematic and conventional stylistic analysis, it
announces an approach to reading—a *form* of intelligibility—
that is more in keeping with contemporary critical practice. Long
and painstaking elaboration and illustration are evidently in
order before such an analysis of discourse can serve as the
ground for extensive interpretive formulations. My own speculative remarks on the structured play of ideological discourse and,
ultimately, in defense of abstraction as a discursive practice
doubtless illustrate the perils to which the impulse to interpret
sometimes leads us. I have chosen, however, to present my reading of La Rochefoucauld as it stands in the hope that the critical
movement animated and anticipated by the *Maximes* and the
Réflexions will bear witness to the artistic vitality and intellectual
stimulus of these austere and eccentric works.

The interest and assistance of many friends and colleagues at
Yale and Cornell have made the completion of this book a re-
warding experience. For material assistance I am beholden to two
institutions, the College of Arts and Sciences at Cornell for a
summer research grant, and the Camargo Foundation in Cassis,
France, for a semester in residence during which work on the
manuscript was completed. I should like to single out three
individuals for their special contributions: Jean Boorsch, who
proposed that I work on La Rochefoucauld and whose criticisms
of the earliest version of the manuscript were the primary guides
in the design and composition of this book; David Grossvogel,
whose assistance included invaluable encouragement as well as
incisive critical questions and suggestions; and my wife, Catherine
Porter, who helped at every step along the way. I also wish to
thank the editors of *Yale French Studies* and *Diacritics* for per-
mitting me to adapt here portions of articles published in their
journals, and Bernhard Kendler of Cornell University Press and
Jeanne Duell for their invaluable editorial assistance.
Above all, I shall remember the composition of this book as

coinciding in time with the last years of Jacques Ehrmann, my teacher, thesis director, colleague, and friend. His exemplary courage in the face of death, like his formidable intellectual honesty and acumen, will remain an undying inspiration for those who worked with him. Jacques would have placed little stock in the sentimental gesture of a dedication *in memoriam,* but I know that he took pleasure in the knowledge that his friends would pursue, however inadequately in his absence, the serious work of elucidating and appreciating the play of literature.

PHILIP E. LEWIS

Ithaca, New York

concluding in time with the last years of Jacques Ehrmann, my
leader, co-director, colleague and friend. His exemplary
remarkable intellectual
honesty and earnest will remain an undying inspiration for
those who worked with him. Jacques would have placed little
stock in the sentimental gesture of a dedication in memoriam,
but I know that he took pleasure in the knowledge that his
friends would pursue, however inadequately in his absence, the
arduous work of elucidating and appreciating the play of literature.

PHILIP E. LEWIS

New Haven, New York

❖

La Rochefoucauld

1 A Problematic Work

Just as reading La Rochefoucauld has almost always meant reading the *Maximes*, reading the *Maximes* has almost automatically entailed reflecting on the nature of the maxim, on its status as a genre or type of statement. The apparently simple question—what is a maxim?—leads into a tangle of complex problems in La Rochefoucauld's work. To each answer, to each notion or definition of the maxim, corresponds a particular image or interpretation of La Rochefoucauld. Examining divergent perceptions of the *Maximes* and various accounts of the maxim proposed by La Rochefoucauld's readers will provide a convenient introduction to the problematics of reading his work.

The Maxim in Literary History

While the habitual designation of La Rochefoucauld's acknowledged masterpiece as "le livre des *Maximes*" might suggest that it is composed of more or less uniform, well-defined statements, the complete title—*Réflexions ou sentences et maximes morales*—properly reflects the impression of variety and discontinuity conveyed by the book. One might submit, however, that the longer title confuses more than it clarifies, for the conjunction *ou* may either equate or differentiate *réflexions* and the succeeding terms. Thus two readings are possible: the book is composed of reflections that are, in reality, short statements of moral import; or the book combines two kinds of writing, reflections and short statements of moral import. Neither reading is a felicitous introductory characterization of the text. On the one hand, its dominant mode of statement would better be labeled observation or affirmation than reflection. On the other hand, regardless of their length, most of the statements are surprisingly difficult to reduce to a strictly moral intention. If, then, the title allows the inference of some positive moral value to be gleaned from the work, the text itself seems to disconnect the essentially synonymous terms *maxime* and *sentence* from their conventional meaning of precepts, or rules of conduct.[1] Whereas La Bruyère, in the preface to *Les Caractères*, refuses to apply the term *maxime* to his work on the grounds that he lacks the requisite legislative genius for writing moral

---

1. J. Dubois and R. Lagane, *Dictionnaire de la Langue française classique*, 2d ed. (Paris, 1960), p. 317. La Rochefoucauld himself generally used the term *sentences* rather than *maximes* in referring to his work (they can usually be employed interchangeably). Huet claims (incorrectly) to have obtained a change in title from *Maximes* to *Réflexions morales* after having noted that "one called maxims only those truths known through natural reason and accepted universally; whereas the propositions contained in this work were new, little known, and discovered through the meditation and reflection of an insightful and clairvoyant mind" (quoted by Pierre Kuentz, ed., La Rochefoucauld, *Maximes*, Les Petits Classiques Bordas [Paris, 1966], p. 180). Given that La Rochefoucauld's own use of the term *maxime* was questionable and unusual, Sister Mary Francine Zeller's laborious attempt to establish historical distinctions among a series of terms (proverb, adage, apophthegm, aphorism, sentence, *pensée*, reflection, maxim) seems rather pointless (in *New Aspects of Style in the Maxims of La Rochefoucauld* [Washington, D.C., 1954], pp. 1–14). Throughout this book I have cited La Rochefoucauld's texts in rather literal English translations. Attentive readers will note, however, that I retain the French titles *Maximes* and *Réflexions diverses*, and that, in accordance with the usual practice of La Rochefoucauld's readers, I construe these titles as plural nouns (referring implicitly to the plurality of particular texts in the books as well as to the books per se) which, when they occur as grammatical subjects, require a plural verb. Since this is contrary to the usual convention in English of treating titles as singular nouns, my phrasing may sometimes strike a discordant note, but I hope that use of the French titles will alleviate this impression.

laws, La Rochefoucauld adopts the term while nonetheless desisting from the task of direct moral prescription.

Even a casual look at the text reveals that not all the *maximes* are maxims. The distinction to be drawn here is an agreeably commonplace one that admits of a variety of terms: short/long, esthetically pleasing (*beau*)'/flat, striking/prosaic, concise/discursive, paradoxical/expository, epigrammatic/reflective. Corresponding to the first term of these pairs and squaring with over three-fourths of the 504 *Réflexions ou sentences* is the maxim;[2] to the second term corresponds an awkwardly amorphous category that ranges from the full-fledged essay to the quasi maxim, which is relatively short but lacking in pithiness or finality. The obvious analogy between the language of these nonmaxims and that of the *Réflexions diverses* seems to justify terming the nonmaxims "reflections" and stressing the characteristic punch, or *frappe,* of the well-honed maxim.[3]

The distinction between paradox and exposition, as set forth by Harold E. Pagliaro, calls for special attention because it correlates only in approximate fashion with the others. The terms of the distinction are said to refer to thought patterns instead of stylistic features. Pagliaro notes, however, that "paradoxical

2. Some rough statistics will suffice to document this point. As generally throughout this book, I use here Jacques Truchet, ed., *Maximes* (Paris, 1967). Workable data on length can be obtained simply by counting the number of lines per maxim (given an average 10.3 words per line): 29 maxims occupy one line each; 250, two lines; 118, three lines; 56, four lines; 23, five lines; and 28, six or more lines. Thus 54 per cent occupy two lines or less; 77 per cent, three lines or less; 88 per cent, four lines or less. Nearly all the four-line maxims possess at least one of the conventional criteria for maxims (*frappe, pointe,* or paradox) to which we can refer, though in the second half of the *Maximes* an occasional text, usually an explanation (that is, a specification of causes), appears rather dry or flat. This observation is, of course, intuitive or impressionistic, and it seems clear that many texts of medium length (thirty to sixty words) would seem good maxims to some readers and not to others.

3. This distinction is employed by Roland Barthes, ed., *Maximes et Réflexions* La Rochefoucauld, Le Club français du livre (Paris, 1961), introduction, pp. xlii ff.; and by W. G. Moore, "La Rochefoucauld's Masterpiece," *Linguistic and Literary Studies in Honor of Helmut A. Hatzfeld,* ed. Alessandro S. Crisafulli (Washington, D.C., 1964), pp. 264–65.

aphorisms rely as much upon the force of style as upon intellectual acuity for their effect,"[4] whereas the so-called expository
aphorism depends primarily upon the presentation of argument.
Such a categorization thus resurrects, with uncommon subtlety,
the irrepressible dichotomy of form (force of style) and content
(argument). To Pagliaro's credit, his analysis carefully disallows
the implication that the reflection, less explosive and more fully
developed, is more truthful or trustworthy than the maxim,
which might be considered more apt to gloss over intellectual
deficiency with stylistic polish. Yet the issue is raised in clear-cut
terms: can the maxim be reduced, in essence, to an identifying
form, or is it the articulation of a distinctive message? Is the
text of the maxim rooted in the practice of a particular style or in
a particular kind of insight?

Although the tenuous opposition of style to substance has long
been suspect, most commentators on the *Maximes* have continued
to qualify the maxim in terms of one or the other, and thus to
view one as the antecedent, if not the cause, of the other. Especially in "traditional" criticism, the maxim has often been
apprehended through loose characterizations of its message,
treated as a recording of experience or as a revelation of the
truth. Lanson, stressing the distinction of the maxim from the
portrait, saw in the latter a reflection on particular experiences
and in the former a "synthesis of experiences."[5] For P.-H.
Simon, the maxim is, rather than a precept, a "sharp and refined
statement in which experience and reflection are condensed so as
to unveil man in the nudity of his nature," thus part of a "collection of clinical entries."[6] So for Lanson, Simon, and many
others, the maxim appears to be an outgrowth of research—a

4. "Paradox in the Aphorisms of La Rochefoucauld and Some Representative English Followers," PMLA, LXXIX (March 1964), 45.
    5. Gustave Lanson, *L'Art de la prose* (Paris, 1911), p. 127.
    6. Pierre-Henri Simon, *Le Domaine héroïque des lettres françaises* (Paris,
1963), p. 182.

vehicle of broader or deeper truth concerning man and his world, an instrument of social and psychological enlightenment. The significance of the loose analogy with scientific research lies in the presupposition that there is *a* truth, unique and definitive, to be unearthed and expressed in formulae appropriate to its nature. For many readers, this presupposition is doubtless reinforced by the maxim's inherent tendency toward abstraction and generalization, associated with the conclusions of experiment or argument.

For others, however, acceptance of this notion of experiential truth—La Rochefoucauld's truth—is conditioned by an important reserve. Although the maxim gives expression to a private and personal truth, it remains, nevertheless, a public and general statement, to be reinserted into a personal dimension, tested here and now, and thereby *verified* by the reader in the light of his experience. Thus the truth for La Rochefoucauld has to be supplemented by La Rochefoucauld's truth for us; the maxim has to be situated in the *present,* in the tense to which its verb is confined. It is instructive to consider several critical statements that uphold this view:

The maxims fix the final state of an experience. . . . The experience has taken place; it has become language; life is henceforth this completed comedy whose quintessence is grasped from afar by a definitive insight. The *Maximes* are written in the present, but in each of them what is involved is an eternal present with no opening onto the future. [Starobinski]

The "instantaneous" or the "pose," in effect techniques to which the choice of the maxim's formula limits him (the writer) and which transmit to us, in brief, contrastual images, the static result—immobilized in a fragment of time and space—of his soundings in the hidden depths. [Mora]

There is a transfer of experience from one level to another, a process of decanting in which the particular gives place to the general which then becomes the possession of all men. [Sutcliffe]

Whether the maxim represents the sum of a lived experience or the fruit of a polite conversation, its verb is nonetheless located within a present of all times that cannot be fragmented. [Secretan][7]

At first glance, repetition of the idea that experience undergoes a transformation or remodulation in language will raise few eyebrows. What does draw attention here, however, is the status of the result: "static, immobilized in a fragment of time and space," the maxim is apprehended in a "present of all times," "with no opening onto the future," as the "possession of all men." Secretan explains that the maxim can succeed in capturing only certain stable moments of duration, in isolating from time "these privileged instants" when the ever-changing being of man can be grasped in its essence. But if generalized experience is immobilized, "de-temporized" experience, has it not then lost the character of experience? Is not essence the antithesis of experience?

Far from reflecting a supposedly experiential foundation, the generalization, through its imposing timelessness, enacts a radical exclusion of the sense of "lived experience." It is necessary to distinguish the instantaneous present, apt to allow readers to participate in the perception that it mediates, from the durative present of the maxim. The latter marks, not the immediacy of the particular moment, but the inaccessibility of an undifferentiated eternity; not the discontinuous character of experience, but the continuity of permanence; not the fullness of presence, but the emptiness of absence. It is in this dimension—otherworldly, as it were—that the maxim can acquire a disconcerting impact, that of an arbitrary sentencing of man to his irrevocable fate by a distant, impersonal judge. Moreover, the gap between the maxim and

7. Jean Starobinski, ed., *Maximes et Mémoires,* Coll. "10/18," (Paris, 1964), introduction, p. 182; Edith Mora, *François de La Rochefoucauld,* Ecrivains d'hier et d'aujourd'hui (Paris, 1965), p. 56; F. E. Sutcliffe, "The System of La Rochefoucauld," *Bulletin of the John Rylands Library,* XLIX (Autumn 1966), 245; Dominique Secretan, ed., *Réflexions ou sentences et maximes morales* and *Réflexions diverses,* Textes littéraires français (Geneva, 1967), introduction, p. xxii.

experience (readers' as well as author's) cannot be adequately represented as a spatial distancing, an effect of perspective. In the passage from the personal to the impersonal, from the temporal to the atemporal, from the presence of experience to its absence, what takes place is nothing less than a movement into another order—that of language as something other than and distinct from lived experience. If, as Starobinski writes, experience has become language in the maxim, it is only at the price of being negated as experience. Its relationship to language, echoing that of the concrete to the abstract, is diaphoric rather than metaphoric.

Thus the maxim is born of negation and separation. To the extent that it compels the reader to experience the unnerving separateness of words, it persists in exerting a disruptive force. While involvement of the reader in the truth of the *Maximes* is an inevitable product of that force, the dynamics of such involvement can hardly be reduced to the act of self-recognition. While a reader may discover in a maxim the truth of his own experience, he will be no less apt to sense that the same maxim overrides conventional orders of truth and, in so doing, challenges his own. Moreover, insofar as the "absolute" truth of the maxim lies within a domain which remains unspecified, the truth of the maxim is itself insecure. In other words, reading the maxim involves a kind of confrontation between the absolute and the relative in which each threatens the other, in which each version of the truth appears in its problematical aspect. However convincing, however telling, the maxim's truth still becomes the reader's problem. The phenomenon in question is designated by Barthes as part of the paradox of the maxim: its generality achieves the most intimate questioning that literature can incite in its reader.[8]

That the reader senses an accusatory interrogation in the authoritative affirmations of the *Maximes* is poignantly illustrated in La Fontaine's fable "Man and His Image." Here the mirror

8. Introduction, *Maximes et Réflexions*, p. xxxv.

image becomes the focal point of the maxim's paradox. To escape from the mirrors that haunt him with his own unbearable image and deflate his self-admiration, a man flees to a remote hideaway in nature. There he encounters, however, an even more disturbing mirror in the clear water of a little stream. His dilemma has an esthetic source: the stream is so beautiful that he has great difficulty in turning away his gaze. The mirror both attracts and rebuffs—like the maxim. The validity of the maxim/mirror analogy extends to Man in general, to *our* soul and *our* faults:

> Our soul is this man in love with himself;
> All these mirrors are the foolish acts of others,
> Mirrors, the legitimate painters of our faults;
>   And as for the stream, it is the one
> Which everyone knows, the book of *Maximes*.[9]

The *Maximes,* then, constitute an indictive mirror. Reflecting an ambiguous light on the man who scales their generality down to his particular situation, they call forth both adherence and resistance, identification and self-exclusion. Because of the tension that this process generates, La Rochefoucauld's "sentences" are often perceived as instruments of provocation, quickly become objects of reflection and debate; their appeal includes the intellectual pleasures to be garnered through the criticism a maxim elicits. In "Man and His Image," the application of the mirror image to the *Maximes* is exceptionally incisive because the fable does more, as a tale, than play upon man's ambivalent relationship to the unsettling maxim/mirror; it also represents the futility of attempting to escape from the perception of self-revealing truths. Just as the insecure hero of the fable fails to find a self-protecting refuge in the seemingly innocent, impersonal truths of nature, the insecure reader will find no reassurance in the apparently definitive truths of the maxims. In depicting the discovery of still another mirror, one that is pain-

9. *Fables* (Paris: Garnier, 1962), I, 2, pp. 44–45; the rather literal translation of this final stanza is my own.

fully attractive, the fable warns of what is to be found in the *Maximes:* not a resolution of man's problems, but a forceful renewal of the interrogation to which life subjects him.

The mirror image exposes the truth of the maxim as a reflection: it is not *the* truth, but an image of truth, at once perfect and distorted, that the maxim captures and projects. To escape from that image, as the egotist of the fable sought to do, would be to turn away from reflection—from the trial of self-awareness—and thus to dismiss the problem of truth, which stems precisely from its shaping in thought and language. To face the problem, however, to threaten self-love with self-perception, is to contemplate the image that the stream reflects, to examine the form discernible in the maxim. By its very title, "L'Homme et son image" posits a conjunction of substance and form which is inescapable in the search for truth. Only by observing his image—by engaging in the process of reflection in which he can perceive the formality of his being—can man begin to grasp the truth about himself. No less than the mirrors of society and nature, the maxim confronts us with the necessity of recognizing this critical conjunction, of approaching the *truth* that it reflects through the perception of its form.

The accumulation of maxims in a collection, like the accumulation of lines and verses in a long poem, gradually evokes the presence of what Lanson called an "artistic mold," a pre-existing regulatory pattern that is apt to place its distinguishing mark upon a variety of ideas and unite them in tone, if not in substance. Studying the variants which often preceded the finished maxim tends to confirm the priority of form in the gestation of the text, for a very high degree of calculation and rigor seems to be channeled into the achievement of concision. "The *Maximes* of La Rochefoucauld, at least in their form, are an exercise, the most conscious and the most punctilious, the most accomplished."[10] The fact remains, of course, that the study of variants

10. Marcel Arland, *La Prose française* (Paris, 1951), p. 390.

does not in itself disclose the form in question, which can be apprehended only in the result of the exercise of compression. The most serious attempts to represent the maxim as a form, those of Barthes and Kuentz, grow out of their attentiveness to the types of relations that prevail among the linguistic elements of the finished sentence.[11]

Before it is read, the maxim makes its appearance in the two-dimensional space of the printed page. Arising abruptly between two patches of white, two moments of silence, "it *is* immediately, in its entirety, in its heart, in its very death, since one grasps in a single movement its beginning and its ending."[12] Conclusion without introduction, "the maxim is a short-circuit,"[13] the epitome of the *pensée détachée,* removed not only from any context but, in its inviolable literality, from ordinary language itself: "The maxim, on the contrary, *fixes* meaning in a terrible immobility; it does violence to language to the extent that it abbreviates. Does the maxim seek to persuade, to convince, or to repeat? No, it *speaks,* without however displaying the intent of communication."[14] Here Barthes is dramatizing a kind of formal alienation inherent to the maxim, personified as an autonomous oracle, self-satisfied, holding all of its relationships unto itself. In connecting words that seem strangely abstracted from specifiable referents, the maxim invites concentration upon the arrangement of its terms, diverts attention from the process of representation to the art of verbal combination. Citing Mme de Lafayette's hesitation between two possible combinations— "Unfaithfulness is pardoned, but is not forgotten" and "Unfaithfulness is forgotten, but is not pardoned"—Kuentz ventures this forthright acknowledgment: "The maxim, as one can see, pre-

11. Kuentz's introduction obviously leans heavily on Barthes, just as Secretan repeatedly borrows points from Starobinski. Nevertheless, Kuentz's approach is very much his own, and he differs considerably from Barthes in his use of a relatively traditional, "descriptivist" idiom and in his presentation of the maxim's form within the framework of genre studies.

12. Barthes, p. xxxiii.

13. Kuentz, p. 30.

14. Barthes, p. xxxiv.

sents itself fundamentally as a form."[15] Barthes carries the conclusion one step further, arguing that a critical reading of the
Maximes should seek to surmount the patternless diversity of
subjects and the tendency to read into the maxim one's personal
truth by giving up the traditional study of development, composition, evolution, or content. Instead he proposes to adopt "a
criticism of the sentencial unit, of its design, in short of its
form."[16]

Barthes takes care to distinguish between the external appearance and the internal structure of the maxim, since an important
step in his analysis will be the disclosure of a discontinuity within
the maxim that in some sense parallels its disconnection from discursive language and/or from the rest of the *Maximes*. As the
variance in description of the external and internal forms indicates, the two discontinuities in question are of divergent orders.[17]
To describe the maxim in its external aspect is almost inevitably
to resort, after a minimum of analysis, to metaphors of hardness
and brilliance, most commonly, that is, to images drawn from
jewelry, which depend upon a global perception of the maxim as
an object or upon the impression that it makes on the reader.[18]
Such a description tends to consecrate, as it were, the fixity of
the text in an essentially static context of isolation. In this respect,
each maxim is unique, a text in itself, a stylistic gem immedi-

15. Kuentz, p. 31.
16. Barthes, p. xli.
17. We can represent schematically the analogy that Barthes seems to be
erecting: maxim : *Maximes* : : basic elements of the maxim : maxim; or,
language of the maxim : ordinary language : : key words of the maxim :
whole sentence. But in both Barthes and Kuentz this is rather sketchily
outlined, and the significance to be attached to the nominal parallelism of
these discontinuities is not at all clear, although there is evidently supposed
to be a sort of reinforcement of the maxim's exclusivity and immobility
within its texture.
18. Secretan, pp. xxix and 264, calls attention to the abundance of images
drawn from jewelry, as had Kuentz before him (p. 41). His own use of
musical analogies is notable; for example, "An orchestrated meditation, the
Maximes hardly illuminate the past any more than does a symphony"
(p. xxii). And cf. Kuentz, p. 39: "this artist who orchestrates his 'variations'
on a few simple themes."

ately perceived as literature. The formal independence of each
text within the work makes it necessary to seek to relate the
maxims on the basis of their internal structure, to look for a
pattern or paradigm around which the text of each maxim is
constructed.

Inside the typical maxim Barthes identifies a few stable elements (notably substantives, acting as the cornerstones or building blocks of their sentences), autonomous in their own right,
coexisting in an essentially passive, fixed relationship, typically
mediated by the inert intransitive, *to be*. From this standpoint,
the maxim appears to be the epitome of essentialist discourse. In
opposition to Barthes's superstructural representation, we may
consider the compositioning of particular elements as it is grasped
in the reading of the text. The process of reading allows no less
for setting off than for offsetting the discontinuity of textual
elements. It constructs an articulation that takes the form of a
linear movement and invites recourse to another order of description designed to translate a modulation, frequently to
analogies with music. In connecting its elements the maxim defines its own tightly structured internal context in contradistinction
to the disjointed literary framework in which it appears. In
contrast to the static image of the text as a radiant jewel, an im-
mobile configuration of component parts, the maxim's terminal
thrust toward a *pointe* evokes a dynamic image, the moving form
of a *crescendo*. The incommensurability of the ornamental and
musical metaphors draws attention to the relative primacy of the
internal structure of the text. Since the dynamics of composition
accounts for the maxim's decisive impact—its effect of solidity
and inviolability—it is precisely upon the form governing the
articulation of the text—its movement toward immobility—that
the study of its structure inevitably focuses.

Interpreting the *Maximes* will ultimately require us to examine in detail the problem of describing the form of the maxim.
The key issue to be resolved pertains to the designation of basis
units and relationships: does the maxim develop around one or

more elemental models or core forms? And if it does, how do we identify and interpret the core form(s)? By virtue of its simplicity and generality, Barthes's "structuralist" description seems to offer a model solution. Barthes unequivocally posits a kernel sentence of the form NOUN-COPULATIVE-NOUN as the fundamental axis or achetype of the maxim, which would then constitute a relationship of equivalence (most characteristically, the restrictive identity of the form "X is *only* Y"). The maxim can then be defined as a variation upon the semantic relationship of synonymy. The analyses of Serge Meleuc, based upon generative grammar, renew the attempt to treat the maxim as a *transformation* performed upon a basic proposition.[19] Whatever the core form or kernel sentence that is identified, this approach to the corpus of propositions that we can label bona fide maxims (on the basis of the loose criteria previously noted) opens up the possibility of accounting for a particular maxim in terms of the generative principles underlying its formation. Specifying these principles would allow the critic to go beyond the particular text and grasp the collective or contextual logic of the *Maximes*.

The decision to approach the maxim through its form rather than through its message does not necessarily predetermine the significance of form itself. Nonetheless, accentuating the function of form tends to subvert our commonsensical ideas about the experience of language. In Voltaire's now canonical view, the language of the *Maximes* exemplifies the signal virtue of expressing ideas with concision: "This little collection was read avidly; it accustomed one to thinking and to enclosing his thought in a lively, precise, and delicate turn."[20] On the other hand, the search for concision, coupled with a variety of salient stylistic devices that serve to surprise, to stimulate, or to shock, achieves a paradoxical result: the prose of the maxim eventually calls attention, not to the idea expressed, not to the nimble turn of the

19. Meleuc, "Structure de la maxime," *Langages*, no. 13 (March 1969), 69–99.
20. *Le Siècle de Louis XIV*, quoted by Kuentz, p. 187.

thought, but to itself, as language *on display*. For Barthes, the
tendency to bring out the spectacle of language through the
outburst of a *pointe* relates the maxim to poetic and archaic
language: with them it shares a propensity to manifest through
striking antitheses the basic mechanism of meaning, which
emerges from an opposition of terms.[21] The poetic/archaic texture of the maxim reflects an experience of language in its
density, in its originary force. Not merely a transparent vehicle
of expression, language is opaque, self-assertive, an instrument
of action. Speech is an immediate embodiment of thought and
feeling, a mythic act; writing, a graphic substance and a mode
of impression:

The maxim is a poem before its time (and is its faraway origin not
sacred, divinatory?); it presents to us in a single movement the
word and the nothingness from which it emerges, into which it returns; it is then, in a sense, wonder at pure language, its substance, its
power, its miracle; for the maxim language is not yet the *expression,* so to speak, of a thought, an argument or an intention, it is
not pure transparency, the extended movement of a progressive
adaptation to reality; it is an almost sacred object, very close to these
magical words that open up the supernatural and subject it to man:
speaking within a closed form participates both in the order of the
sacred and in the order of the poetic, which were originally the
same; it is this archaic function that the maxim recaptures, despite
the civilized, rational character of the classical society in which it
reappears.[22]

In Barthes's analysis, the analogy of maxim and poem mediates the integration of formal and thematic modes: "Like the
lyric poem, the maxim is a way of singing certain obsessions,
variously termed themes or subjects. . . . "[23] In the articulation
of the poet's chant, the form of the maxim assumes a predominant role in the activity of expression itself. Insofar as the funda-

21. Barthes, p. lxii.
22. Ibid., pp. xxxii–xxxiii.
23. Ibid., p. lxxvi.

mental relation of the restrictive identity corresponds to the mental structure of the poet, it functions as an obstacle, an *imposition* of form that reduces expression to the monotonous repetition of the same essentialist equation. Their allegiance to form—what Barthes terms a "radical choice of Literature"—confines the *maximes* to the process of denunciation; it precludes moving beyond a nihilist dilemma into a dialectical solution that certain maxims, by invoking the interaction of opposites, anticipate.[24] There is, then, nothing innocent or impartial about the structural notion of the maxim, which influences the reading of the text quite as decisively as a preconception of its message. To single out, in the texture of the maxim, the formal, poetic necessity of certain elements—words, rhythms, sounds, combinations, syntactic patterns—is to underscore what the writer experiences as the necessity or autonomy of language. The object or experience that would have been expressed becomes, in the maxim, a language to be spoken, an experience of the Word. Apprehended as form, the maxim proclaims the pre-emptive power of language.

However imperious, the form of the maxim by no means excludes the dimension of expression. Even if the *maximes* could be completely reduced to the ritualistic chant of obsessions, they would fulfill an expressive function, would ex-pose and transmute their themes through the process of denomination. Barthes's interpretation clearly allows for the coalescence of form and theme while supposing the primacy of form. But this formalist supposition remains strictly methodological, leaves intact the difficulty of perceiving the relationship of form to theme, of attributing logical or existential priority to one or the other. An attempt to resolve this problem underlies the interpretation of La Rochefoucauld by Starobinski, whose thematic approach implicitly rejects Barthes's equation of themes with the writer's

24. Ibid., pp. lxxiv–lxxv. Most of the discussion of form and expression into which Barthes's interpretation leads is drawn from my article, contrasting Barthes and Starobinski: "Language and French Critical Debate," *Yale French Studies*, no. 45 (Dec. 1970), pp. 154–65.

obsessions and instead sifts out of the subject matter of the *Maximes* the components of an acute analysis depicting the desperately tragic human condition.[25] Thus constituted on the level of perception, that is, directed at the consciousness that expresses itself in the text, Starobinski's interpretation develops an account of La Rochefoucauld's commitment to the form of a maxim. By treating the allegiance to form as the achievement of a solution, admittedly precarious, to the moralist's problem, the critic effectively tempers the notion according to which form acts as a determinant obstacle in the *Maximes*.

Noting early on a significant correspondence between the willful disorder of the *Maximes* and the internal discontinuity of man, between a punctual, fragmentary, paradoxical writing and the diversity and contradiction of human existence, Starobinski supposes forthwith that the object of the moralist's reflection determines the form that it takes: "The discontinuity and the breaking-up of being impose their law and their rhythm on the moralist who describes them."[26] Subsequently, when he takes up what might be termed the theme of form, he calls attention to the "wordly" role of form as a refuge, a last resort: "For he who has shown the nothingness of man, 'wordly' life can continue only in the concern for a form, it being well understood that this form could only be arbitrary and gratuitous, unrelated to a despair for which it offers no remedy."[27] The function of form, then, is to "counterbalance the darkness of the content," not to suppress it. The form in question, which one constructs with words in accord with an "esthetics of expression," develops in its own order, one in which man is the maker of his own values. The fundamental value, which constitutes the order of language as a "human milieu," is the freedom that man discovers only in language,

25. Jean Starobinski, "La Rochefoucauld et les morales substitutives," *NRF*, nos. 163–164 (July/Aug. 1966), pp. 17–34, 211–29.
26. Ibid., pp. 22–23.
27. Ibid., p. 212.

wherein he can create a second self, a "being of language," coinciding with and depending upon the form in which he communicates. This "substitute being" appears in the relational order linking the abyss of passions in man to his latent humanity, that is, it expresses itself in the audible relation of man's nature to his language.

If an esthetics of expression seems unusually transparent in Starobinski's reading, it is not simply because he represents the maxim as an expression of La Rochefoucauld's thought, and thus envisages the writer's work as the free manipulation of the resources of language in the service of his ideas; it is also because Starobinski finds in those ideas the justification for the writer's commitment to form, so that *both* theme and structure, thought and language, are eventually treated as expressions. For Barthes, however, the maxim does not simply *express* La Rochefoucauld's thought, it *is* his thought, which is realized only as the text takes form. Writing is the medium of thinking, and form is no mere esthetic garment, for it describes the relationships that govern meaning. To the extent that his language and his work escape from his manipulative control and affirm their own "personality," the writer effaces himself in them and exists only through them, as he is spoken by them.

Insofar as the maxim, in Barthes's terms, "speaks La Rochefoucauld," it ceases to translate his experience and becomes that experience; it is the achievement of art that takes unto itself the experience of the writer (as a writer) and transposes it directly into the texture of language—as if the author loses himself in his language so that this language can "express" him or, more precisely, *state* him, in its *impression,* as directly and completely as possible. Situating the enunciation of maxims in a social context, Starobinski ascribes a comparable experience to the *honnête homme* who devotes himself to a spirited conversation: "He gains a new existence, a second manner of being, in which his being depends on the form in

which he communicates. He coincides with this form at the
very instant in which the form is invented."[28] In communication with others, this willful dependency on form offers a
refuge from the revelations of descriptive discourse. Protecting
the "being of language" from being grasped except as language, it serves to suppress the problem of (self-) expression,
or rather overlays the darker elements of expression with the
dominant surface of lustrous form.

Ambiguities in the *Maximes*

Whether the emphasis falls upon expression or impression,
on theme or form, both aspects of language—material and
referential, phonological and semantic—are always distinguishable in literature. Whence the inescapable ambiguities of literary language:

Literature is the language that becomes ambiguity. . . . Ambiguity
is there struggling with itself. Not only can each moment of language become ambiguous and say something other than what it says,
but the general import of language is uncertain, for one does not
know if it expresses or represents, if it is a thing of if it designates
the thing; if it is there to be forgotten or if it only makes you forget
it in order to be seen; if it is transparent because what it says means
so little or if it is clear because of the exactness with which it speaks,
obscure because it says too much, opaque because it says nothing.[29]

With exceptional insistency, the *Maximes* renew and evince
such ambiguity. The text of each maxim breaks out of the
continuum of silence only to return rapidly into it; the gathering movement of the text from beginning to end has the effect
of reinforcing its global fixity; the statement that shocks and
unsettles nonetheless offers the comfort of secured knowledge,
yet the definitive affirmation of the particular maxim is but
relative to the ongoing process of critical reduction, which can
only be halted arbitrarily; the exposure of dark truths sets the

28. Ibid., p. 218.
29. Maurice Blanchot, *La Part du feu* (Paris, 1955), pp. 342–43.

stage for the upward valuation of form, so that artistic perfection eventually connotes the sobriety of the underlying message. From every standpoint, the maxim is perceived as an
ambiguous, paradoxical discourse, and as the maxims accumulate in a collection, it is a deepening and intensification of this
ambiguity that the *Maximes* invite us to weigh.

In its most comprehensive outlines, the ambiguity of La
Rochefoucauld's writings comes to light in the context of a
broad, relatively superficial, but clearly indispensable reaction
to the view that La Rochefoucauld's art and outlook represent
the epitome of simplicity, clarity, and good taste. As represented by W. G. Moore and Jean Starobinski, the opposite view
stresses the *complexity* of La Rochefoucauld, a complexity
born of deep penetration into the variety and confusion of
human motives and natural causes.[30] Advancing similar observations, Mora calls La Rochefoucauld "a master of ambiguity,"[31] remarking upon the apparent contradiction between
the changing, unstable image of man and the relentless attempts at stringent elucidation in the *Maximes*. But of course
there is no simple contradiction between elucidation and the
object of elucidation: a lucid exposition of human ambiguity
is perfectly conceivable, but problems arise when ambiguity
seems to enshroud lucidity itself. Starobinski's study carefully
brings out, from La Rochefoucauld's perceptions of man, both
an abrupt simplicity and an overwhelming complexity; by virtue of their juxtaposition the work is all the more complex,
all the more difficult to analyze in terms of logical priorities.
To see the problem in its full extent, it is necessary to distinguish the sources of ambiguity within the work from the various ambiguities attributable to the work as a whole.

30. Moore, "La Rochefoucauld: Une Nouvelle anthropologie," *Revue des
sciences humaines* (Oct.–Dec. 1953), pp. 301–10; Starobinski, "Complexité de La Rochefoucauld," *Preuves*, 135 (May 1962), pp. 33–40 (this
article is integrated into Starobinski's introduction to the "10/18" edition of
the *Maximes et Mémoires*, pp. 12–23.
31. *François de La Rochefoucauld*, p. 37.

As we have noted, the initial and principal source of ambiguity is man—or Man, treated as a species endowed with a human essence. In fact, it is often difficult to imagine that the Man behind the generic *on, nous, les hommes* even approaches the absolute generality of mankind's archetype. Barthes comes very close to identifying the man of whom La Rochefoucauld writes with the author himself, with a powerless aristocrat and intellectual whose vision is limited to the masculine world of his caste. In many of his pronouncements on man, we sense, with Barthes, an evident lack of concern for the variety of social conditions and for psychological heterogeneity. This narrowing of context and import, which the idiom of impersonality makes quite difficult to gauge, implies a partial, unstable perception of the human condition. At the same time, it remains clear that the frame of reference for La Rochefoucauld's writings extends beyond his class and his epoch. The context of his observations is problematical precisely because its scope is not uniformly general and at times remains indeterminate.

In what appears to constitute a refutation of Barthes's suggestion that La Rochefoucauld's concentration upon the generality of the species entails a summary disregard for individuality and diversity, Starobinski argues that an acute awareness of variety and dissimilarity precedes and sustains the recourse to generalization. He bases this argument on texts in which difference can be regarded as the dominant theme:

There are as many diverse species of men as there are diverse species of animals, and the men, with respect to other men, are what the different species of animals are among themselves and with respect to one another. [Réfl. IX, "Du rapport des hommes avec les animaux"]

Perfect valor and absolute cowardice are two extremes men seldom reach. The space in between them is vast, and contains all the other types of courage: among these there is no less difference than among faces and temperaments. [Max. 215]

Starobinski's commentary: "Real man, if we seek to define him, will be found in 'the space that is in between,' this vague space, this doubtful place that is interposed between opposing virtues, between pure values."[32] In this ill-defined territory where no absolutes can properly qualify man's existence, what must be recognized is the unlikelihood that a universal definition of Man will prove to be valid for the individual: "It is easier to know man in general than to know one man in particular" (Max. 431).[33] La Rochefoucauld betrays no confidence that either the general or the particular can actually be apprehended, and his analysis reveals the universality of some human motivations no less than the unique psychological disarray of each individual. Lying somewhere within the ambiguous relationship of the general to the particular, the impersonal subject (*"on,"* and the like) of La Rochefoucauld's dicta subsumes a tripartite frame of reference: a man in his individuality, men in their diversity, Man in his universality.

Nonetheless, both the *Maximes* and the *Réflexions diverses* tempt their readers to overcome their disparate structures by constructing an image of the man whose vicissitudes they depict. As Jean Rousset has demonstrated, it is possible to extract a concept of man—"l'Homme de La Rochefoucauld"—from the *Maximes* by elaborating point by point La Rochefoucauld's refutation of the classical idea of man.[34] One can challenge

32. Introduction ("10/18" edition), p. 18.
33. Starobinski seems to stretch the point when he suggests that in this maxim La Rochefoucauld finally recognizes "the impossibility of defining man in general terms; more precisely, the impossibility of a universal definition of man which is valid for the particular man" (introduction ["10/18" edition], p. 19). In the text, it is not a question of impossibility, but of relative difficulty, and in one sense the problem is not at all the *applicability* of general knowledge but the fact that general knowledge alone is applicable, the particular being accessible solely through a necessary conceptual distortion (cf. Max. 106). See also W. G. Moore, "La Rochefoucauld et le mystère de la vie," *Cahiers de l'Association internationale des études françaises,* 18 (March 1966), p. 107.
34. "La Rochefoucauld contre le Classicisme," *Archiv für das Studium der Neueren Sprachen,* 180 (1942), pp. 107–12. The gist of the argument is that La Rochefoucauld's analyses *nullify:* (1) the unity of man, bereft of a

this rather mechanical analysis by citing maxims that involve
the eminently classical theory of *honnêteté*. Yet elsewhere
Rousset is on solid ground when he connects the theme of
human inconstancy, prominent throughout La Rochefoucauld's
work, with the baroque vision of the preclassical period.[35] The
recurring expressions of this hackneyed theme seem, however,
to reinforce the difficulty of apprehending human nature, of
representing Man at all. The same is true, moreover, of another
leitmotif of baroque literature, the theme of contradiction:
"Imagination could never invent as many and varied contradictions as nature has put into every person's heart" (Max.
478). Paul Bénichou's commentary could hardly be more decisive: "These contradictions are the last word on human nature, its deepest definition; what one finally finds in man is a
sort of undifferentiated emotivity, which can have contrary
actions as its external manifestations."[36] In effect, the contradictions are nothing more than the external manifestations of
this undifferentiated affectivity, which is a kind of internal
chaos devoid of any fundamental ground or mainspring. Even
self-love, the infamous egocentric impulse and all-purpose explanatory principle, is enshrouded by a realm of dark mystery.
At the heart of self-love the unceasing succession of passions
and vices (see Max. 10, 11, 191, 195) gives rise to an analogy
with the ebb and flow of the centerless sea.[37] La Rochefoucauld
similarly associates the image of the sea with love, which, like
self-love, "is subjected to the reign of words,"[38] as if the
opaque world of others that one encounters in love were but

---

central source of stability; (2) man's freedom to control his passions; (3) the
power to civilize nature through reason; (4) the ability to maintain the
ascendancy of mind over heart; (5) man's sociability, his capacity to live
in harmony with others.

35. *La Littérature de l'âge baroque en France* (Paris, 1965), pp. 43, 226.
36. *Morales du grand siècle* (Paris, 1948), pp. 99–100.
37. Cf. Moore, "La Rochefoucauld: Une Nouvelle anthropologie," p. 309,
and "La Rochefoucauld's Masterpiece," pp. 268 ff.; cf. Corrado Rosso,
Virtù e critica delle virtù nei moralisti francesi (Turin, 1964), pp. 3–4.
38. Secretan, introduction, p. xxviii.

a mirror of one's own internal opacity. The groping descent of the imagination into affective life seems to parallel the eye's descent into the depths of an ever murkier, fathomless sea. On this point nearly all recent commentators agree: far from reaching the root constituents of a coherent ontology, La Rochefoucauld's seemingly endless analyses open onto the fundamental disorder of human nature, onto an emptiness, a deficiency, "the lack of being," "a dizzying nothingness,"[39] the impossibility of making any definitive, irreducible statement about the essence of Man. Examining the consequences of portraying man at the mercy of his passions, Antoine Adam notes that the search for coherence and spiritual unity becomes unjustifiable and falls by the wayside; thus he affirms that, from an ethical standpoint, "the *Maximes* eventually lead to a radical ambiguity."[40] In metaphysical terms, this "radical ambiguity" can be ascribed to the search for an essence that does not exist, to the attempt to ground explanations upon a shifting, erosive foundation.

Against the background of the theme of contradiction, it is necessary to distinguish a second source of ambiguity within La Rochefoucauld's work—the coexistence of conflicting explanations. To understand that man is a seat of inconstancy and contradiction, we need only to recognize that a host of changing influences forever assails him from within and without, propelling him into the midst of a manifold determinism. Man is driven both by his own indomitable self-love and by the brute forces of nature. The menace to human understanding results from the differing implications of these two influences: "To say that virtue exists is sometimes, for La Rochefoucauld, to say that impressive actions hide the motives of self-interest, sometimes that they are necessitated by external influences and

39. Starobinski, "La Rochefoucauld et les morales substitutives," p. 34; Barthes, introduction, p. lxxii.
40. *Histoire de la littérature française au XVII⁰ siècle*, IV (Paris, 1958), p. 98.

thus devoid of merit."[41] The explanation based upon self-love allows a moral condemnation that explanation grounded in natural causes excludes. If this contradiction is to be overcome, a problem of perception that preconditions the act of judgment must be resolved: how does one tell whether, in a given instance, self-love or a natural cause determines action, whether man is partially or fully subjected to uncontrollable forces? And a corollary problem concerning self-love: how and when (if ever) does it differ from simple instinct, become something more than a mere agent of physical determinism? It would be imprecise to trace these questions to the ambiguity of a partial determinism. La Rochefoucauld's explanatory formulae are wont to be straightforward and uncompromising—"fortune and disposition ['humeur'] rule the world" (Max. 435). Yet the concrete operations of these ruling agents seem to remain inaccessible, unpredictable, visible in their broad outlines but, as the terms *fortune* and *humeur* (evoking the bodily humors as well as temperament) suggest, resistant to precise, logical comprehension—"the capriciousness of our dispositions is still more bizarre than that of fortune" (Max. 45). While this exceedingly abstract comparison does nothing to clarify the problematic relation between *fortune* and *humeur*, it provides more than just a derogatory comment on man's peculiarities or inconsistencies. For the invocation of fortuity, improbability, and chance also entails an acknowledgment of the ambiguous, incomprehensible phenomena in man's world that bring him face to face with his limited, inadequate understanding. Here

41. Paul Bénichou, "L'Intention des *Maximes*," in *L'Ecrivain et ses travaux* (Paris, 1967), p. 5. Bénichou's article provides an admirably straightforward formulation of this problem (pp. 5–16), which, in diverse readings of La Rochefoucauld, is seen to arise from the opposition of two principles of debunking: "the system of self-love and the idea of an indifferent and capricious causality" (p. 9). Starobinski also offers an explicit treatment of the problem in terms of an "overdetermination of our acts and our qualities" (introduction, p. 17), viewing it as a sort of "radicalization" of the sense of contradiction (p. 21). Francis Jeanson offers an earlier and more uncompromising formulation in *Lignes de départ* (Paris, 1963), pp. 76–80.

the distance between the general and the particular is compounded by the gap between observation and explanation.

To the conceptual ambiguities discernible in the representation of man and in the explanation of his conduct, it is appropriate to add a third source of ambiguity within the work: the presence of obscure, anomalous, or polyvalent meanings. Within this category, a composite of particular cases rather than a single, underlying ambivalence, a fairly wide range of semantic dilemmas is encountered. To begin with, it seems undeniable that a part of the maxim's piquancy derives from a deliberately cryptic quality: "The art of the maxim is not just that of abbreviated speech; *ainissomai*, says the Greek, 'speaking in enigmas.' "[42] Beyond a mere enigmatic effect, however, a real conceptual obscurity can be glimpsed in "umbrella words" or in "mots-mana,"[43] in abstract notions such as interest or vanity that include or explain so much that they verge on equivocation. Seeking an explanation for this rather surprising obscurity within the framework of La Rochefoucauld's outlook, Moore finds a remarkable number of texts that attest to a veritable sense of mystery and suggest that a certain awareness of ambiguity permeates the articulation of La Rochefoucauld's thought. Upon determining that certain maxims can be read either as denunciations of egotism or as applause for a bold aspiration, Henri Coulet adopts a similar approach.[44] In La Rochefoucauld's insistence upon the inextricable intermingling of truth and falsehood, virtue and vice, and so forth, he finds a definition and a justification of this ambiguity. On the level of the *Maximes* as a whole, the extreme case of semantic ambiguity occurs when one maxim appears to contradict another; such an opposition intensifies the crucial problem of their rela-

---

42. Kuentz, introduction, p. 30. See also Rosso, *Virtù*, p. 5, who suggests that the enigma results involuntarily from the search for concision.

43. Moore, "La Rochefoucauld et le mystère de la vie," p. 106; Barthes, introduction, p. 66.

44. "La Rochefoucauld et la peur d'être dupe," in *Hommage au doyen Etienne Gros* (Gap, 1959), pp. 108–11.

tive priority, which results from the fragmentation of texts within the work.

To glimpse the broad ambiguities enshrouding the attempt to interpret La Rochefoucauld's works as an ensemble, it suffices to consider the formidable variety of moral and ideological positions to which they have been linked: pessimism, Epicureanism, Jansenism, Stoicism, anti-Stoicism, Pyrrhonism, materialism, naturalism, determinism, formalism, nihilism, immoralism, heroism, voluntarism, and still others.[45] Such an enumeration speaks for itself. In the moral sphere, it seems particularly futile to go on searching for a proper denomination among the various conventional positions that La Rochefoucauld might have picked up from his contemporaries. Not only do the *Maximes* lie, as Kuentz has noted, at the crossroads of of several moral doctrines;[46] both the *Maximes* and the *Réflexions diverses* display a degree of circumspection (perhaps the refusal to take any position on religious matters is the most intriguing case) that suggests that their author sought actively to avoid being identified with a given point of view, possibly with an eye to distinguishing his work from others and marking it as personal. Although the *Réflexions diverses* do include a fairly direct presentation of the doctrine of *honnêteté* (in some respects a doctrine of circumspection), the fact that they were not published by La Rochefoucauld might simply reflect a preference not to be associated with a recognizable position that would settle him into a particular niche in literary or intellectual history. At any rate, since the standard procedures of synthetic description cannot do justice to a work that sternly throws them into question, it is understandable

45. It seems pointless to provide a reference for each of these terms. Ample verification of the tendency (reductionism, so to speak) exemplified by the words in *-ism* may be found in Corrado Rosso, "Processo a La Rochefoucauld," *Critica Storica* (Nov.–Dec. 1963), pp. 638–53, (Jan.–Feb. 1964), pp. 27–48.

46. Kuentz, introduction, p. 30.

that Truchet concludes his introduction to the *Maximes* by claiming for La Rochefoucauld the *right* to ambiguity.

If one could nevertheless discern a definite, though eccentric, orientation in these works, the impossibility of categorizing them would represent a relatively superficial ambiguity. Uneasiness in reading them results from the suspicion that beneath their evasive quality is a conscious rejection of the unequivocal, that ambiguity is the necessarily unwritten doctrine of La Rochefoucauld. What Kuentz terms a "work without a message"[47] may be read as a work on the impossibility of a message; as such it would be entirely consistent in omitting any direct statement that this impossibility is its message and that only messages remain possible. Freed from the requirement of unitary coherence, La Rochefoucauld's position can be represented as a juxtaposition of two or more outlooks, for example, the destruction of all human pretension and the construction of the society of *honnêteté;* a lucid morality appropriate both to a cynic and to a martyr; an approval of two courses, heroic action and tranquil acceptance of man's fate; the intellectual simultaneously challenging, expressing, and accepting his society; cohabitation in the moralist's conscience of the "qui suis-je?" and the "je suis sordide";[48] and so forth. Yet such alternatives continue to pose, for the reader, a critical problem. Given, for example, a juxtaposition of wholesale critical destruction and the theory of *honnêteté,* does the criticism extend to the concept of *honnêteté* and prove it unworkable, or does *honnêteté* constitute a positive response that confronts and actively moves beyond the results of the passive observer's debunking? The prominence assumed by these diverse possibilities may depend largely upon the reader's perspective: "Depending upon the

47. Ibid., p. 40.
48. These examples are drawn, respectively, from Starobinski, "La Rochefoucauld et les morales substitutives," pp. 211–12; Mora, *François de La Rochefoucauld,* p. 67; Secretan, introduction, p. xviii; Barthes, introduction, p. lxxviii; Bénichou, *L'Ecrivain et ses travaux,* pp. 17–18.

angle from which one looks at them, the *Maximes* are a manual of *honnêteté* and a treatise of pessimistic psychology, but also a sort of sober and elevated poem bearing the accent of a nostalgia for glory."[49] This remark by a critic studying heroic elements in the *Maximes* is symptomatic: to recognize the ease with which one can read a given perspective into the *Maximes* (or the *Réflexions diverses*) is to edge away from an arbitrary interpretation, to respect the experimental character of the work. In the end, it may be just this experimentality, the ambiguity grounded in the unstated exclusion of definitive interpretation, that becomes the critical object of interpretation.

The Trials of Fragmented Reading

The ambiguities of La Rochefoucauld's writing clearly lay open and amplify the problematics of reading. From the outset, the reader of the *Maximes* is apt to be acutely aware of his freedom to react to the texts in his own way, in accordance with his own situation and temperament.[50] Standing alone as a provocative statement, the maxim clearly makes special demands upon the reader, requiring a search for meaning and frequently educing a judgment on its truth-value. The more poignant, paradoxical maxims also tend to elicit, at least from many readers, an intuitive or emotive response, an immediate reaction to which notions of the maxim's impact or *effect* have commonly been linked. Pagliaro refers forthrightly to "nervous response, and the disturbance that precedes cognition";[51] other critics prefer metaphorical allusions to the wounds inflicted upon the reader's spirit, or to the feeling of moral paralysis engendered by the *Maximes*. It is clear, in any case, that the initial bite of the maxim increases both the difficulty of and the necessity for intellectual detachment.

49. Simon, *Le Domaine héroique*, p. 182.
50. Cf. Sainte-Beuve, "M. de La Rochefoucauld," *Portraits de femmes* (Paris, 1862), p. 269.
51. "Paradox in the Aphorisms of La Rochefoucauld," p. 46.

In reviewing the opinions gathered by Mme de Sablé in 1663, Truchet points out that several readers reacted more favorably once the first impression had worn off.[52] The *Maximes* were clearly viewed from the outset as an occasion for dialogue (in some cases direct dialogue with the author); they offered their readers a kind of stimulus or reference point for reflection and discussion. In the "Discours sur les *Réflexions ou sentences et Maximes morales*," a defense of La Rochefoucauld's work by Henri de La Chapelle-Bessé and placed after the "Avis au Lecteur" of the first edition, we find a remarkable passage on the role of the reader offered in answer to the objection that the *Maximes* are marred by obscurity:

The obscurity . . . is not always the writer's fault. *Les Réflexions* . . . must be written in a compressed style which does not allow for making things as clear as would be desirable. These are the first strokes of the painting: clever eyes will indeed see here all the subtlety of the painter's art and the beauty of his thought; but this beauty is not made for everyone, and although these strokes are not filled in with colors, they are no less the touches of a master. One must then take the time to penetrate the meaning and the force of the words, the mind must move across the whole spectrum of their meaning before settling down to the formation of a judgment.[53]

Staking La Rochefoucauld's claim to an initiated audience (an antecedent of the Stendhalian elite) of kindred spirits, Bessé also contends that the intelligent reader should naturally formulate the appropriate restrictions for excessively general state-

52. Jacques Truchet, "Le Succès des 'Maximes' de La Rochefoucauld au XVII⁰ siècle," *Cahiers de l'Association internationale des études françaises*, 18 (March 1966), pp. 125–37.

53. Quoted in the Truchet edition of the *Maximes*, p. 279. In addition to a magnificent presentation of texts that allows us to study the development of the *Maximes* from edition to edition over a fifteen-year period, this edition includes an exceedingly valuable collection of documents, much excellent commentary, the best available edition of the *Réflexions diverses*, and, in the editor's introduction, a remarkably judicious and surprisingly thorough account of La Rochefoucauld's life. In citing maxims, I use Truchet's notations, MP for posthumous maxims and MS for maxims from previous editions omitted in 1678.

ments. The reader must not simply perceive the picture passively in its broad outlines; his task as reader is *supplemental*
to the author's task, involves an active contribution to the completion of the maxim's meaning. Although the degree of La
Rochefoucauld's complicity in the development of Bessé's
apology cannot be determined, his correspondence and the
opinions gathered by Mme de Sablé prove that he fully appreciated the interpretability of his work and was willing to
provide his own commentary on particular maxims.[54] No doubt
he also understood the risk of depending so heavily upon the
reader, who may give in to the temptation to impose extraneous
views upon the *Maximes*. Indeed, when Helvétius ascribes La
Rochefoucauld's notion of interest to a utilitarian outlook, or
when a modern commentator extrapolates from the clouding of
the vice/virtue distinction to a strained association with sur-
realism and the exposure of "traditional ethics gaping at the
Absurd," it seems that the interpreter's risk—of becoming the
dupe of the very text that accentuates his interpretive license—
is just as great.[55] The reader should not dismiss lightly the
"Avis au lecteur" of 1665, which ironically advises him to
presume that none of the maxims will concern him personally.
This liminary warning establishes the appropriateness of the
ironic detachment assumed by the author. Moreover, the reader
eventually realizes that his exclusion from the moralist's criticism is at times far from ironic. Some maxims are not merely
inapplicable to him but evoke an experience apparently beyond
his grasp, meaningful only to superior beings. In other words,
if the reader feels personally implicated by some maxims, he is
alienated by others, and it is this troubling variation between
inclusion and exclusion that makes his relationship with the
work unstable and problematical.

54. See, in the Truchet edition, letters 6 (p. 546) and 47 (pp. 589–90).
55. Helvétius, extract from *De l'Esprit* quoted in the Pléiade edition of
La Rochefoucauld (*Oeuvres complètes*, ed. L. Martin-Chauffier and Jean
Marchand [Paris, 1964]), pp. 740–41; and Mora, *François de La
Rochefoucauld*, p. 67.

In order to get a better hold on the elusive *Maximes*, one can try to situate them alongside the *Réflexions diverses* and the *Mémoires*.[56] While it is fair to maintain that these works should be read as an ensemble, by no means does it follow that they must be forced into a coherent framework, within which the *Maximes* should then be read as one part of an integrated whole. The *Mémoires* and the *Réflexions* evoke, respectively, a turbulent world of Cornelian heroism and a stable world of polite society;[57] the *Maximes* incorporate reflections of both worlds, but nothing hints at a synthesis of the two, or even a transition from one to the other. When maxims appear in the *Mémoires* (where there are very few) and in the *Réflexions*, they bear little kinship to those of the *Maximes* because they are located in an expository context that tempers their sting and controls interpretation. To ascertain the unique independence of the *Maximes*, it suffices to try reading them as we read La Rochefoucauld's other works, in a continuous movement through the text. It is significant that such a continuous reading cannot work. We can agree with Barthes that there are at least two ways to read the *Maximes*, "selectively or in order," haphazardly or consecutively, personally or critically.[58] While, at a certain level of appreciation, the book should be read "in flashes, as it was composed,"[59] it is still necessary to undertake the step-by-step critical reading at some point. The alternative

56. La Rochefoucauld's complete works also include, of course, the extant portion of his correspondence. Apart from the letters concerning the *Maximes*, it is fair to say that the majority provide a relatively uninteresting documentation of La Rochefoucauld's incomparable *politesse* and have negligible literary value. Among the exceptions is in particular the remarkable letter to his son, the Prince of Marcillac (Pléiade edition, pp. 658–60).

57. Although there is considerable variation of perspective in the *Réflexions*, which occasionally revert to a historical viewpoint that could allow for a certain association of the work with the *Mémoires*, the overall tenor of the two works seems to me to justify this distinction. Cf. W. G. Moore, "The World of La Rochefoucauld's *Maximes*," *French Studies*, VII (Oct. 1953), 334–45.

58. Barthes, introduction, pp. xxi–xxxii.

59. Jean Rostand, "La Rochefoucauld," *Hommes de vérité*, 1st series (Paris, 1942), p. 213.

would be to renounce completely the effort to exclude emotional reactions and contrived or impressionistic interpretations, to give up the search for synthetic understanding.

Yet even this systematic reading, however painful or monotonous in comparison to a random search for engaging insights, cannot be continuous, for each blank space separating one maxim from the next interrupts the flow of thought before it picks up momentum, laying out an open dimension of time and space for reflection, for weighing the maxim just read, for returning to a *table rase* before reading the next one. Only at the price of reduced comprehension can any reading gloss over the intrinsic autonomy of each maxim. Within the *Maximes,* there is no explicit sign of one maxim's relation to others, no trace of the gradually developing comprehension that emerges as we read through a poem or a page of prose. Never acceding to that advancing confluence of statements which creates a unified context of meaning, the *Maximes* generate a multiplicity—perhaps irreducible—of coordinate relationships. The absence of visible priorities leaves intact the virtual equivalence in import of each maxim. What, then, determines the nature and the coordinates of the relationships among maxims? This is the principal responsibility La Rochefoucauld leaves to the reader. We are free to organize the maxims as we see fit, and tempted to proceed beyond coordination, to suppress the disjunction of the texts and treat them as if they were convertible into a single expository statement, as if each maxim were a part of one long reflection.

Reading consecutively from maxim to maxim is a revealing exercise. The reading process both suggests that the discontinuity of the book is incontrovertible and develops a certain sense of intratextual relationships. In their unwavering isolation, all the maxims have to be isolated from something. As Kuentz observes, since it is a general phenomenon, the *solitude* of the maxim underlies the *solidarity* of the maxims, each of which maintains its inviolate fixity over against a shifting ground

(*fond chatoyant*) toward which a search for conceptual unity
in the *Maximes* inevitably leads.[60] But can one get a hold on
this shifting ground? Starobinski has argued forcefully that it
will not be apprehended by the traditional, albeit uneasy groping toward "La Rochefoucauld's secret" (presumed to be hidden within but reflected by the *Maximes* and perhaps more
overtly evidenced by the *Mémoires*).[61] Perhaps, as Kuentz
suggests, that "shifting ground" does confer upon the *Maximes*
a dialectical cast, but the fact remains that most readings that
aim to discover the ultimate coherence of the whole work hardly
proceed in terms of a dialectic. For neither the *Maximes* nor
the *Réflexions* lend themselves to a dialectical reading. Both
tend to elicit a reading according to subjects, that is, a topical,
classifying reading that proceeds by identifying themes—as if
La Rochefoucauld's recourse to a table of subjects at the end
of the *Maximes* makes up for the lack of ordering noted in the
"Avis au lecteur" and provides the key to the book's underlying structure.[62] The occasional groupings of maxims on the
same subject reinforce the tendency to read in terms of fixed
notions or essences and to formalize a set of stable relationships among them. To move beyond thematic or structural
similarities to a concentration upon conflicting theses is not to
move out of a stable frame of reference into a dialectical process. As Bénichou's study shows, the resolution of contradictions does not take place within the movement of the work. It
is envisaged by the reader in terms of a logically ordered intellectual itinerary that the *Maximes* subtend or by reference
to a deep-seated experience apt to generate conflicting, but
actually complementary, responses.

60. Kuentz, introduction, p. 40.
61. Introduction, pp. 24–25.
62. Rosso grounds his study of the *Maximes* in this topicality, relating the
maxims according to their themes and arranging the themes in a more or
less logical order. He does not appear to be concerned with the problem that
results from the possibility of arranging the themes in various ways so as to
produce variant interpretations, but does not try to deny a certain arbitrar-
iness in his own interpretation.

Nevertheless, Kuentz's strategic association of the *Maximes* with a dialectical process embodies a valuable corrective insofar as it allows for perception of the particular maxim both in its textual independence and in its intratextual relativity. Many readers have sought to resolve the problem of relating the maxims among themselves by asking whether some text or texts within the book do not dictate a method for understanding other maxims or delimiting their validity. In considering, for example, the implications of this maxim—"Our actions are like set-rhymes, which everyone connects with whatever he pleases" (Max. 382)—can one go so far as to argue that La Rochefoucauld presents a résumé and a refutation of his book?[63] Are all the explanations of human conduct in the *Maximes* to be written off as expressions of the author's personal inclinations? Does a maxim on the difficulty of judgment (for example, Max. 170) or knowledge (Max. 106) undermine La Rochefoucauld's own statements? Over and over, critics have accused La Rochefoucauld of refuting himself, of falling prey to his own system. "It is true that the sword which the moralist brandishes so ardently ended up by striking him too, but he paid no attention to that."[64] "The misfortune is that this mistrust does not spare the author either: in fact, it is he who is touched first and most seriously."[65] Or, by going one step further and indicting, as does Jeanson, the intellectual's bad faith,[66] one can argue that La Rochefoucauld deploys his (in)famous lucidity in an abortive attempt to immunize his own reflection, to guarantee its invulnerability by setting it in ironic detachment from the context to which it refers.

At this point, there is no need to reiterate the obvious objections to reducing La Rochefoucauld's work to an expression of his personal disillusionment and resentment. As Bénichou

63. As does Emile Deschanel, *Le Romantisme des classiques,* 3d series (Paris, 1888), p. 60.
64. Rosso, *Virtù,* p. 28.
65. Coulet, "La peur d'être dupe," p. 112.
66. *Lignes de départ,* pp. 71–107.

points out, to insist on extending La Rochefoucauld's practice of critical negation to his work is to assume that his negations constitute nothing more than a drawn-out exercise in self-destruction, in nihilism.[67] In order not to treat prejudicially the positive elements of his thought, such as the approbation of *le naturel,* it is necessary to posit the initial relativity, the experimental character of his destructive criticism, which may or may not acquire the force of an absolute. Perhaps a more elementary point should be stressed, one that suggests no bias in favor of an ultimate "wisdom" attributable to the moralist. If *Maxime* 382, or another like it, refutes the *Maximes,* it also refutes itself unless we can prove that it has a special, irreducible character that the other maxims lack. Just as we admit that the first principle of any system of thought is self-validating and does not turn back upon itself, we have to admit that the maxim does not invalidate itself, that each maxim has absolute value within its sphere. The problem is to determine its relative value with respect to the other maxims. This is the heart of what we shall term the problem of fragmentation.

Throughout this introduction to the problematical aspects of reading La Rochefoucauld, various consequences of formal discontinuity have been in evidence. La Rochefoucauld's apparent disdain for a logical ordering of the maxims, which becomes more pronounced in the later editions, cannot be equated simply with a disdain for pedantry or for bourgeois attitudes. Similarly, treating the fragmentation of the *Maximes* as a function of the artist's desire to maintain variety and avoid *ennui* does not materially advance our understanding of its effective properties as a function in the overall meaning of the work. Once it is granted that the maxim naturally resists being drawn into an externally defined context, that some of its aphoristic charge would be drained off if it were readily apprehended as a point in an argument or a component of a system,

67. *L'Ecrivain et ses travaux,* pp. 3–4.

it remains necessary to consider the context—of which discontinuity is an integral part—which is formed by the work, necessary to ask whether or not an implicit argument or latent system is present in the *Maximes*. In short, confronting the finished work, the reader still has to interpret its fragmentation.[68]

One glaring consequence of fragmentation in the *Maximes* is the difficulty of discussing the structure or architecture of the work. From the few critics who have considered the question the essential lesson to be drawn indicates primarily that the first edition (1665) shows some definite signs of an ordering process: "The 1665 volume begins with a definition, or rather with a sketch in bold outline, of self-love and its effects on our passions; then it goes into detail and attacks, one after another, the principal virtues."[69] Whence the notion of a battle order, of a gathering assault on the bastions of virtue, that has been considerably muted and distended by 1678: "La Rochefoucauld must have realized at some point that the element of surprise was more suitable to his esthetics of fragmentation than a systematic development."[70] An *esthetics* of fragmentation would presumably dictate a kind of ordered disorder, a subtle, not necessarily rationalistic structuring that subordinates thematic development to a predominantly esthetic logic.

In the lone serious study of the architectural problem published to date, Truchet undertakes to elaborate this kind of argument. In regard to the first edition, La Rochefoucauld did not hesitate to admit that a concerted ordering of the maxims would have been desirable: "I do then agree that it is unfortunate that they have appeared without having been com-

68. It should perhaps be noted that the *Réflexions*, although endowed with the nominal continuity that stems from discursive language, also manifest a significant degree of discontinuity. As constituted by La Rochefoucauld's editors, the text presents a disparity of subject matter and an absence of transition or logical arrangement that disallow a linear or sequential perception of the work's coherence.

69. Edmond Dreyfus-Brisac, *Le Clef des maximes de La Rochefoucauld* (Paris, 1904), p. 28.

70. Secretan, introduction, p. xix.

pleted and without the order which they should have had."[71]
Truchet contends that La Rochefoucauld nevertheless could
not have failed to recognize in advance that the order of the
maxims conditions their effect. In support of his affirmation
that "the order is subtle, but it exists,"[72] Truchet develops two
main points: (1) the constant variation of sentence structure
probably reflects an attempt to delight the attentive reader who
reads straight through the book and appreciates new combinations, delicate deviations from an established pattern, and recurrent surprise or shock effects; (2) the "battle order" of the
Maximes can be adduced by noting in their order of appearance
the groupings of four or more maxims on the same subject:
(*a*) edition of 1665—"amour-propre, passions, modération,
constance, orgueil, bonheur et malheur, fortune, amour, amitié,
esprit, tromperie, finesse, louange, mérite, vertus, vices, valeur,
reconnaissance, bonté"; (*b*) edition of 1678—"passions, orgueil, amour, amitié, esprit, finesse, louanges, mérite, vertus,
vices, valeur, reconnaissance, élévation."[73] The reduced number
of groupings underscores the greater dispersion of subject
matter and diminished concern with thematic ordering in the
final edition. Thus the expansion of the collection confers relative primacy on the motif of variation, with formal variations
freely complemented by thematic ones. Yet the central thrust of
the attack remains evident: "His great enemy is man's continuing ignorance of his own motives,"[74] or, as La Rochefoucauld
prudently declared in the "Avis au lecteur" of the first edition,
"Self-love the corruptor of reason."[75]

As far as the order of the groupings of maxims is concerned,
it is clear that the most significant change after 1665 is the
omission of *amour-propre* at the beginning of the sequence.
Otherwise, the order remains substantially the same, especially

71. Lettre au Père Thomas Esprit, in the Truchet edition, p. 578.
72. Introduction, p. xxii, note 5.
73. Ibid., p. lx.
74. Ibid.
75. Truchet edition, p. 270.

since most of the groupings omitted from the second list have simply been diminished by suppressions. What is not clear is the thread of logic that might be followed through either series of subjects. If one grants that self-serving ignorance undergoes a constant siege and that this provides an underlying thematic unity, it remains difficult to see a unified progression in these series of themes, within which we can only distinguish groupings of groupings (for example, *amour-propre* + *passions; modération* + *constance; esprit* + *tromperie* + *finesse*), just as the groupings of maxims are noticeable in the larger grouping, the *Maximes*. Sister Mary Zeller adopts the rather incongruous device of graphing the 504 maxims according to their 149 (!) themes, thereby uncovering seven major thematic clusters (in order: *passions, orgueil, amour, amitié, esprit, louange, valeur*), all of which occur prior to Maxime 230. The zigzags of her chart verify clearly, if anticlimactically, the pronounced dispersion of the second half of the collection, which obviously contains fewer clusters and varies themes more capriciously than the first half, reflecting a decided trend toward diffusion as the work expanded from edition to edition.[76]

Zeller suggests that from her charts, tables, and observations "there arises the suspicion that the work of La Rochefoucauld is a carefully constructed collection of consciously thought-out and worked-over ideas, and not a mere selection of random thoughts propagated by *un bel esprit*."[77] Overlooking the unlikely opposition of La Rochefoucauld to the *bel esprit* and the axiological implications of Zeller's suspicion, one might draw from her data almost the inverse of her conclusion—that the *Maximes* are not, as a collection, carefully constructed, and that, if the clusters of maxims are taken as single thematic elements (a dubious procedure), the succession of themes represents little more than a random arrangement. If Truchet's "subtle order" is to be found through a linear reading as he suggests, it will necessarily involve the play of stylistic varia-

76. Zeller, *New Aspects of Style,* pp. 148–49.
77. Ibid., p. 147.

tions, and here again the concept of a random alignment, or, in a more literary parlance, of a baroque labyrinth, seems much more appropriate. In his response to the factual question concerning order in the *Maximes*, Barthes is entirely correct in affirming that there is no logic in the succession of the maxims, that the logic and the thematic of the work cannot be found in its extension and must be sought in a dimension of depth.[78] The work calls for a reading that attempts to respect its linear discontinuity. Our task as readers is to ask what order, if any, underlies the surface disorder, or more generally, of what the fragmentation of the *Maximes* is a function or a sign.

If no direct answer to the question of fragmentation can be ventured until after studying the *Maximes* in depth, at least it is possible to formulate some hypotheses to be kept in mind in the course of this study. One hypothesis would place heavy emphasis on the autonomy of each maxim, representing the *Maximes* as the direct, unmediated practice of a method. Each maxim would be a blow administered by a demolition expert whose basic task is ex-posing or de-structuring; or it would be a vehicle of discovery, apt to translate in its logical estrangement the infinite dissimilarity that analysis uncovers and that the scholarly treatise would distort through systematic presentation. As a rhetorical instrument, the maxim would reflect a conservative attitude toward language use, an unwillingness to accept the logical (or epistemological) restraints and implications of a discursive language or a systematized position. Set in the context of such linguistic reticence, the language of the maxim, as it suddenly erupts from the wisdom of silence, would resound with unprecedented iconoclastic force.

A second hypothesis concentrates on the object of the moralist's perception, assuming a correspondence between the disorder of the *Maximes* and the disorder of man. The latter would be describable only by a succession of zigzags, of scattered insights whose dissociation would reflect the disintegration of consciousness, the discontinuity of emotive phenomena,

78. Introduction, p. xxxviii.

or the groundless structure of the personality. As a third and final hypothesis, one might take the discontinuity of the *Maximes* to be a sign conveying their ultimate message. In this case the truth of the work would not merely be transmitted through its disjointed form; rather, it would reside in the disjuncture, in the process of meaning which is embodied by the juxtaposition of fragments to be grasped in their mutual distinctiveness. Thus the continuing accumulation of fragments would bear witness to the function of dissociation and deferral in the generation of meaning. As with the first hypothesis, the *Maximes* would pose an implicit challenge to the legitimacy of searching for truth in discursive continuity.

These hypotheses are not mutually exclusive. None of them requires the assumption, frequently accepted without reflection, that La Rochefoucauld's thinking undergoes a deliberate fragmentation only after having been conceived as a unified, systematic position. Each of them assumes, instead, that our task in reading La Rochefoucauld may consist less in reconstituting such a unified position than in grasping the significance of discontinuity within a work in which it is a fundamental and irrepressible phenomenon. For in the last analysis, it is not possible to subsume the problem of fragmentation in the critical context in which it arises, in a study grounded upon the genesis of the *Maximes* as a literary work and the related development of the author's intention to forgo logical arrangement. The finished work does not acquire its meaning and significance directly and exclusively from the process of production; it assumes the existence of a definitive text, and as such, the work calls for an appreciation which, beyond the purview of causal explanation, situates it in relation to its "effects." In other words, prior to undertaking an interpretation of the *Maximes*, it is important to recognize that a critical reading of the work takes its roots in—and therefore will ultimately return to—the conscious effort to read the maxims *as fragments*.

2 The Psychology of Self-Love

The first edition of the *Maximes* opens with a long reflection on self-love, originally published in a collection of exemplary prose by various authors in 1660. Inasmuch as Maximes 2, 3, and 4 also concern self-love, La Rochefoucauld apparently deemed it advisable to present this theme as the starting point and nominal cornerstone of his work. As Truchet points out, the earlier texts of the *Maximes,* including the copies distributed by Mme de Sablé in 1663, did not open with this concentration on self-love and tended to accentuate the falseness and impurity of virtue as their dominant themes.[1] Consequently, one suspects that La Rochefoucauld, prompted by the general response to Mme de Sablé's poll of opinions, recognized the perils of challenging the value or authenticity of Christian virtues and sought to allow the reader to associate the *Maximes* from the outset with a virtuous denunciation of egotism.

The use of the concept *amour-propre* in the "Avis au lecteur" of the first edition certainly bears out such a thesis. Not only does La Rochefoucauld point out that the *Maximes* treat self-love as a corruptor of reason, he warns the reader against per-

1. Jacques Truchet, ed., *Maximes* (Paris, 1967), introduction, pp. xxi-xxiii, and see the note on p. 133. One might simply represent this alteration as a transfer of emphasis from observation to explanation, a shift in focus from effect (falsity of virtue) to cause (self-love).

mitting self-love to intervene in his judgment of the maxims against it. Any condemnation of the work, he observes, can be dismissed as just another manifestation of hidden interest, pride, and self-love. Thus this preface explicitly stresses, over and beyond the importance of the theme, the argumentative utility of the concept: self-love can serve to explain (away) almost all human conduct. Little wonder that literary history has traditionally attributed precisely this role to self-love in the *Maximes*.

Recent commentary on La Rochefoucauld generally takes issue with the long-standing consensus on the import of self-love. The initial advantage of the traditional view stems from its decisive simplicity: "No one had yet formulated such a rigorous theory of self-love. . . . La Rochefoucauld's primary merit is thus to have reduced the multiplicity of our faults and apparent virtues to unity." "La Rochefoucauld makes self-love the pivot of his whole philosophical system. . . . The entire book is just the application of this general principle to particular cases."[2] These views offer a veritable explanation of the *Maximes*, one that the book itself is said to provide by specifying its theoretical principle. In order to accept such an explanation, it is necessary to assume that self-love is a stable, predictable, universally applicable factor, that its nature is clearly observed or postulated by La Rochefoucauld, whose maxims invariably concern, if not self-love per se, its manifestations. Arguments against traditional views of the role of self-love have disputed this assumption by drawing upon either of two simple observations: (1) there are many maxims apparently unrelated to the notion of self-love; (2) the *Maximes* construct an image of self-love that disallows the use of the notion as a fundamental principle.

Some critics have sought to contest the presumed centrality of self-love in the *Maximes* by pointing out that other themes (such as love, friendship, passion) appear with much greater

2. Henri Gaillard de Champris, *Les Ecrivains classiques* (Paris, 1934), p. 227; R. Grandsaignes d'Hauterive, *Le Pessimisme de La Rochefoucauld* (Paris, 1914), pp. 10–11. Affirmations comparable to these abound in writings on La Rochefoucauld until the 1930's.

frequency.[3] The statistical argument is surprising, however, since direct reference to the theme has little to do with determining whether or not the elaboration of a given maxim is governed by the concept of self-love. At this level of analysis, the primacy of self-love is, in fact, undeniable, simply because so many of the major themes (*intérêt, vanité, orgueil, amour, amitié, passion, esprit, habileté, vertu, vice*)[4] can be readily understood as the manifestations or appearances of self-love: "There is no passion in which love of self rules so powerfully as in love . . ." (Max. 262); "The passions are only the diverse tastes of self-love" (MP 28); "Interest is the soul of self-love . . ." (MP 26); "Pride, which is inseparable from self-love . . ." (Réfl. 18, "De la retraite"). But there are exceptions (among them, *défauts, qualités, merite, ennui, fortune, hasard, humeur*) that preclude the supposition that self-love is "omnideterminant," and suggest that other, independent causal factors and valuational principles come into play: "However great the advantages provided by nature may be, it is not nature alone, but fortune with nature that makes heroes" (Max. 53); "Knowing how to put mediocre talents to good use is an art which gains admiration and which often earns more renown than true merit" (Max. 162); "If the various effects of boredom are carefully examined, it will be found that boredom occasions more failures in our duty than self-interest" (Max. 172); "There are disgusting people who have merit, and others who are pleasing even with their faults" (Max. 155). Maxims such as these clearly entail no direct application of a theory of self-love, which, for example, would tend to discredit the notion of "true merit" by depicting it as "an effect of self-love," forcing us to speak of *what we call* true merit. On the other hand, it suffices to consider the implications of various warnings on the cleverness and disguises of self-love (such as

3. Truchet, introduction, pp. lviii–lix; Edith Mora, *François de La Rochefoucauld* (Paris, 1965), pp. 54–55.
4. See the tables in Pierre Kuentz, ed., *Maximes* (Paris, 1966), pp. 34–37.

Max. 4, 236, 247, 39, 246, 253, MS 1) in order to see that
the traditional position might be rehabilitated if formulated in
more radical terms.

How might a theory of self-love account for a maxim on the
power of fortune? Only by according self-love a role in the
elaboration of the text. In this case the operation of the principle in the *Maximes* would no longer entail simply the unveiling of egotistical motives by a disinterested observer. On the
contrary, the observation on the power of fortune, or any other
affirmation, could not be disinterested; it would have to reflect
the unconscious or undeclared influence of self-love, never absent from the exercise of human perception. That self-love may
be present when it appears to be absent comes to light in the
description of its ultimate ruse, which is to turn against itself:
"Thus there is no cause for surprise if it sometimes joins hands
with the most rigorous austerity and thereby participates braz-
enly in its own destruction, for at the very moment that it
courts ruin in one place, it finds renewal in another; when you
think it is giving up its pleasure, it is only suspending it for a
while or shifting to another one, and even when it is vanquished
and you believe you are rid of it, you discover that it returns
triumphant in its own defeat" (MS 1).

Given the propensity of self-love to obtain gratification, like
the saint, through self-denial, we can hardly suppose that observing the power of other forces—"Fortune and temperament
[*humeur*] rule the world" (Max. 435)—will threaten its ascendancy. Far from undermining its position, the occasion for
self-effacement allows self-love to achieve a special delectation,
a feeling of pride growing out of the magnanimous recognition of limits, a sense of ultimate triumph that can emerge only
from a struggle with formidable opposition, an anticipation of
exaltation in defeat through the miraculous power of rebirth.
In other words, the opening text of the first edition of the
Maximes suggests that no maxim can be automatically dissoci-
ated from the ruses of self-love, since all human activity is

rooted, consciously or unconsciously, in the all-pervasive force of egotism.

If self-love is treated as the originary center of the *Maximes*—as the intentional force that directs the articulation of the maxim—it becomes necessary to revise the view according to which the *Maximes* are but an application of the stated principle of self-love to particular cases. Each maxim would be, rather, an expression of self-love in action, would serve as its voice, as its channel toward consciousness. And maxims that specifically refer to self-love would constitute a special case incorporating both expression of the active principle and application of the intellectual principle, would function as the self-consciousness of self-love. The personification of this fundamental faculty would, then, preside over the composition of the *Maximes:* the book would represent an exercise in self-satisfaction, a kind of virtuoso performance in which self-love knowingly appears in all its guises in order to reap all possible pleasures, not the least of which comes from self-revelation, from the vainglorious proclamation of its power. At the same time, the dynamics of self-satisfaction would coincide with those of interest, with a strategy of self-protection dependent upon self-exposure. The consciousness of self-love conceives of its interest as the cultivation and preservation of desire, and thus erects barriers against both the unrestrained expression of desire, which threatens self-destruction, and inexpedient conflict with stronger forces in nature and society. Instead of simply applying a theory of self-love, the *Maximes* would also embody its dialectic, and the grandiloquent reflection that opened the first edition would have constituted not just an overly explicit announcement of the central thematic but also a self-conscious prefiguration of the work as a whole.

This first glimpse of self-love, however hyperbolic, serves to accentuate the pre-eminent role of personified faculties in La Rochefoucauld's psychology. Ultimately, examining the "problem" of personification will involve taking measure of a major

objection to the moralist's psychologizing: the extent to which
that psychology relies on a contradictory notion of self-love as
a conscious unconscious. At this juncture, however, we must
dispense with a more immediate objection, a form of the logical one mentioned earlier in regard to invalidating the *Maximes*
through the application of a given conclusion enunciated within
the work. Is not the forgoing revision or reinforcement of the
thesis on the primacy of self-love subject to the same objection?
In particular, is it not illegitimate to consider a maxim about
self-love an expression of self-love, to apply the lessons about
self-love to the exposure of self-love? Should one not rather
allow the exposition of egotism to stand unmolested in its own
sphere, a statement of principle disconnected from the actual
operation of that principle?

Here the objection does not hold because of the unique, self-
sustaining nature of self-love. One might dismiss this maxim—
"In jealousy there is more self-love than love" (Max. 324)—as
only an expression or device of self-love, that is, one might
claim that in this maxim self-love is asserting its presence in
jealousy in a weak attempt to draw satisfaction from the otherwise painful experience by converting it into a realization of
one's love for oneself. This would "reduce" the text to just
another instance of self-love's propensity to make the best of
any circumstance. Far from invalidating either the maxim or the
principle of self-love, such an interpretation actually corrobo-
rates them both: self-love takes pride in revealing its ascendancy
over love for others in the experience of jealousy; it discovers
an occasion for affirming itself and confirming a domination that
becomes all the more decisive as that experience becomes self-
conscious. Never do either the *Maximes* or the *Réflexions* suggest that the exposure of self-love can serve to counter its
domination. With compelling consistency, they recognize instead that man's egotism is so deeply ingrained, so indomitable
that only the effort to placate and restrain it can make any sense.
Although retaining conclusively the image of the *Maximes* as

the voice of an enlightened self-love, as the spokesman for *intérêt*, may not be warranted, there is cause to refrain from reducing it, as many have done, to a simple-minded denunciation of egotism.

The exceptional power and resiliency of self-love, as well as its potential for elaborate personification, derive from its dual nature: self as the center of personality, love (wish or desire) as a force or active principle. Through this combination of psychic substance and psychic energy, self-love is able to act as its own object, to take advantage of a built-in faculty of introversion that allows it to thrive even while turning back upon or against itself. Recognizing that the explanatory principle of self-love stands intact when applied to itself and that the personified force of self-love can achieve fulfillment when subordinated to other motivational forces, we can no longer pretend to overturn its primacy in the *Maximes* on the basis of the initial observation that many maxims are not connected with self-love. At least, we can no longer make this type of argument work without ignoring the traditional notion according to which the predominant theme of self-love provides the underlying unity of the work. Instead, it would be necessary to assume that the *Maximes,* contrary to the implicit invitation to envisage the operation of self-love at every turn, do not authorize a universal application of the principle. Clearly such an assumption has to be tested against the representation of self-love in the work, for in the light of the conceptual plasticity of the personified notion, it would be overly facile to take the thematic diversity and formal discontinuity of the *Maximes* as immediate signs of incoherence or disunity. In the last analysis, then, acceptance or rejection of the traditional view of self-love has to be predicated upon a study of the concept and its function.

The long reflection that opened the first edition of the *Maximes* provides the inevitable starting point for this study. As we have noted, however, the status of this distended maxim

is clouded by its omission after the first edition. Moreover,
owing to the baroque nature of the text and its original association with a "circumstantial" literature, there is cause to wonder
if it is not—rather than the product of "a fulgurant vision
which . . . furnished him [La Rochefoucauld] with the raw
material of his succeeding collections"—merely "a rather
frivolous page in its precious style and taste for paradox."[5]
This problem of how seriously to take the reflection can, in turn,
be resolved only through analysis of the text and comparison
with other texts dealing with the concept of self-love. For the
moment, it suffices to recognize that the exceptional stylistic
qualities of the text can hardly be taken as mere bravura.[6]

The text of MS 1 starts out as a definition but moves rapidly
into the framework of a verbal portrait in which self-love undergoes an extravagant personification: "Self-love is love of
oneself and of all things for self; it makes men worshipers of
themselves, and would make them tyrants over others, if fortune
gave them the means. It never pauses for rest outside of itself,
and, like bees on flowers, only settles on outside matters in
order to draw from what suits its own devices." The opening
statement indicates that self-love is not egotism in the narrow

5. Dominique Secretan, ed., *Réflexions ou sentences et maximes morales*
and *Réflexions diverses* (Geneva, 1967), introduction, p. xxvi; Truchet,
introduction, p. xxiii, and cf. p. lv, note 4.

6. For Sainte-Beuve, MS 1 is "an admirable summing-up which is yet to
be refuted; it is a piece worthy of Pascal, of the Pascal of the *Pensées* . . ."
(*Nouveaux Lundis*, V [Paris, 1872], p. 388); W. G. Moore entitles his
article on the text "La Rochefoucauld's Masterpiece," in *Linguistic and
Literary Studies in Honor of Helmut A. Hatzfeld*, ed. Alessandro S. Crisafulli
(Washington, D.C., 1964). For other notable commentary see Paul Bénichou,
L'Ecrivain et ses travaux (Paris, 1967), pp. 9–10; Jean Starobinski, in
Maximes et Mémoires, Coll. "10/18" (Paris, 1964), introduction, pp. 11 ff.;
and Robert Kanters, in La Rochefoucauld, *Oeuvres complètes*, Bibliothèque de
la Pléiade (Paris, 1964), introduction, pp. x–xi. The search for stylistic
effects that is so clear-cut in MS 1 is equally transparent throughout the
Maximes, so that, from a strictly literary standpoint, MS 1 fits admirably into
the collection as a kind of stylistic watershed for the entire work, drawing
attention to the key motifs of variation and metamorphosis by displaying their
coextension in style and theme. Unless otherwise noted, all quotations in the
following discussion will be taken from MS 1.

sense of love confined to oneself, but egoism in a relatively technical sense—desire necessarily conceived in terms of self, self-centered because it can have no other origin, no other frame of reference. "We can love nothing except in terms of ourselves . . ." (Max. 81; see also Max. 339). The domain of self-love embraces everything that may become an object of desire, so that, in principle, it is boundlessly expansive.

Beginning with the second clause of the introductory statement, the portrait develops primarily in terms of the activity of self-love. Working independently, isolated from the men it controls insofar as it exerts a tyrannical influence upon their conscious existence, it encounters frustration only in attempts to expand into control over others (other egoists), into a collective sphere where its influence is tempered by the intervention of fortune. Thus the personification of self-love is not merely a figure of speech destined to vivify the colorless terms of a definition. Growing out of an unmitigated causal relationship— "it makes men worshipers of themselves"—it transforms the subject of a relatively innocuous postulate with respect to the structure of desire into nothing less than *another being,* a resident alien embedded deep within the self and extending a rapacious grasp into and through man's surface personality solely in pursuit of his own mysterious interests. The image of the bee sucking flowers depicts the enactment of self-love's basic impulse: consumption, self-aggrandizement, acquisition in service of an ultimately narcissistic satisfaction that is enhanced and magnified by the projection of desire toward the external world.

Self-love is unique, incomparable, inconceivable: "Nothing is so impetuous as its desires, nothing so hidden as its aims, nothing so devious as its methods; its suppleness cannot be represented, its transformations surpass metamorphoses, its refinements surpass the processes of chemistry." Here the mode of description undergoes a slight, yet critical change. First, the series of superlatives introduced by the negative absolutes "nothing . . . so [much] as" accentuates the motif of exclusivity; the construction of this *superlative* conveys, in effect, the negation of the very possibility of *comparison* to other faculties. Then, as the emphasis shifts toward the motif of transcendence, this impossibility is stated more explicitly by the acknowledgment that the complex operations of self-love escape analogy with even our most sophisticated conceptions. Thus there is a brief movement away from direct representation of self-love (via definition, personification, the bee image) to a perspective that considers not just self-love but also the effort to perceive it. The portrait of self-love turns back upon itself by pointing out that representing self-love has to be a problematical and paradoxical process—comparison to the incomparable, representation of the unrepresentable, or penetration into the impenetrable: "No man can plumb the depths nor pierce the darkness of its chasms: there it is hidden from the sharpest eyes, performing a thousand imperceptible twists and turns; there it conceives, nourishes, and raises, without realizing it, a great number of affections and hatreds. Some of these are so monstrous that, upon giving birth to them, it either fails to recognize them or cannot bring itself to admit having fostered them."

Now the abrupt, unmediated return to direct representation (with "performing a thousand imperceptible twists and turns") poses the paradox squarely and unequivocally: since the depths of self-love cannot be apprehended, how can one write at all of what takes place in those depths? This paradox should not be confused with that of self-love itself, which, for example, combines wildly impetuous desires with unbelievably skillful maneuvers, the stability of a permanent, unassailable stronghold with the perpetual movement and metamorphosis of an unassuageable appetite, humiliating defeat with surpassing victory, and so forth: "It is made of all the opposites; it is imperious and obedient, sincere and deceitful, merciful and cruel. timid and audacious." As Starobinski has noted, such contradictions are only apparent;[7] they serve, by way of example, to reveal the falsehood of appearances, to show that self-love cannot be apprehended directly through its manifestations (masks), which it can vary perpetually. Incisive understanding, then, requires getting down to the level of origin or intention. It is here, in envisaging the depths of self-love's activity, that one confronts the telling paradox, that of the observer, whose confident description of the undescribable seems to imply an unnamed source of omniscience. From here it is but a short step to the attribution of this improbable portrait, viewed as a genre, to artistic imagination (whence Secretan's view of the text as "a fulgurant vision"), or to psychological intuition (or to both), in which case analysis of self-love would indeed give way to the reduction of MS 1 to a verbal fantasy.

The text, however, resists this kind of reduction. It certainly does not suggest that a real penetration into the regions of darkness—the night that covers self-love, and prevents it from perceiving and understanding itself—underlies the portrait. Almost from the beginning, a kind of precautionary recognition of the limits of perception ("there it is hidden from the sharpest eyes") prompts us to view the succeeding expansion of the portrait as nothing more than a hypothetical construct, grounded in the recurrent paradox of the unknowable—that which is known as the irreducibly unknown and which admits solely of metaphorical representation. In sketching the topographical outlines of the activity of self-love, the portrait develops what might be termed an artistic theory, an experimental account designed to correlate the knowable with the unknowable.

In logical terms, this process of "literary theorizing" set in motion by MS 1 involves more than the imaginative pursuit of a dynamic paradox. To play artfully upon the elusiveness of the unknown is to respond to one of man's deepest needs—to engage in an instinctive process of putting the unknowable in

7. Introduction, pp. 12–13.

its place, so to speak, by inventing plausible explanations and by ordering his perceptions of himself and the world around him. Insofar as it satisfies a need to represent more coherently the astonishing flux of appearances that it depicts, the portrait of self-love attests to the cognitive functions of literature, to the rationality informing the play of the literary imagination. The text gives voice to a speculative impulse whose logic is necessarily inferential, proceeding from appearance to underlying principle, from manifestation to invisible source. It is hardly surprising, then, that the conception of self-love reflects the incessant variations of the appearancces for which it seems designed to account.

There is an obvious analogue to such a speculative process in the notion of a psychic unconscious (with which self-love has been frequently equated), which must initially be developed in contrastual relation to the informing model of consciousness. If, as literary history has so often supposed, a theory of self-love serves to confer thematic unity upon the *Maximes,* the elaboration of that theory cannot be regarded as a function of the direct observation of self-love in its essence. The informing model is simply that of ordinary experience: "Its inclinations vary with the varying temperaments which affect it and impel it to seek now glory, now riches, now pleasures. Its objects change in accord with the changes in our ages, our fortunes, and our experiences, but it does not care whether it has several or just one because it sometimes embraces many and sometimes concentrates upon one in accord with the dictates of necessity and with its pleasure." The conjunction of necessity and desire in the concluding phrase ("quand il le faut et comme il lui plaît") evokes an intriguing interplay of determination and freedom. Like any agent caught up in the process of existence, in reaction as well as in action, self-love is always subject to the force of external influences even while exerting its own deterministic force. Any theory of self-love that one can reconstruct in reading the *Maximes* will clearly take into account this action-reaction phenomenon, will incorporate the boundaries and constraints imposed by the dynamics of human experience as a whole. As we examine the developing metaphor of self-love in MS 1, we shall also have to ask what demands and constraints the technique of personification eventually places upon such a theory.[8]

If the darkness of its domicile condemns self-love to ignorance or to vague ideas of its own nature, that darkness in no way prejudices the perception and understanding of what lies outside the indrawn boundaries of the self: "But this thick darkness which hides it from itself does not prevent it from seeing clearly what lies outside itself. In this respect it resembles our eyes, which can perceive everything and are blind only to themselves." This analogy with the eyes indicates poignantly the extent to which the behavior attributed to self-love depends upon its possession of intellectual faculties: perception and consciousness.[9] As desire, instinctively and, it might seem, unwittingly pursuing an object external to itself, self-love seems to mirror the blindness of the eye to its own visual activity. Its

8. It should be clearly understood that the rehabilitation of the traditional theory of self-love by no means entails a claim that MS 1 (or the *Maximes* and/or *Réflexions* as a work) constructs a theory conceived as such by the author, nor does it imply that La Rochefoucauld was intent on exposing a rigid, doctrinaire system. Indeed, the sense of caution and experimentation that I shall note in MS 1 suggests that it should simply be read as a text of theoretical import, as the potential basis or source of a theory to be derived by the analytical reader. The value of this emphasis on theory will, then, be determined by the extent to which it serves to illuminate the moralist's practice.

9. Francis Jeanson initiates his commentary on MS 1 with this surprising declaration: "The first thing to become apparent in this text is that self-love is nothing other than our consciousness" (*Lignes de départ* [Paris, 1963], p. 78). He can then proceed to refute La Rochefoucauld by arguing that consciousness cannot be its own interest, its own self-love. It is clear that Jeanson can manage such a reading only by ignoring the blatantly metaphorical nature of the text, which, in fact, does not treat self-love as consciousness, but as an actor that seems to possess a consciousness. Rather than seeing in this text an attempt to imagine the articulation of passion or instinct from physical stages through mental ones, Jeanson maintains that referring both to "les passions du corps" and to "les passions de l'esprit" constitutes an absolute contradiction.

amazingly efficient apprehension of the external world is paralleled by a relatively deficient sense of its own selfhood: acute consciousness coexists with marginal or imprecise self-consciousness. Envisaged from without, self-love appears submerged in the personality as a kind of contaminated consciousness, incapable of grasping itself as pure consciousness, always pervaded from within by the tenacious drives of brutish desire, never able to perceive its self-centered motives accurately. As a personified impulse, self-love assumes the paradox of the unconscious conceiver, bound to an object that is never its own, that is always furnished by the passions from which this nonpositional consciousness cannot be abstracted: "Indeed, where its main interests and most important affairs are concerned, and the violence of its desires commands its undivided attention, self-love sees, feels, hears, imagines, suspects, sees through everything, so that one is tempted to believe that each of its passions is endowed with a kind of magical power of its own." This sentence, while obviously distinguished by the extraordinary cascade of verbs of sensation and intellection that seems to transpose the frenetic activity of impetuous desire into the realm of consciousness, has two parts that should be measured against each other. In the adverbial phrases introducing the main clause, the perfectly typical characterization of self-love's activity as its *business* ("intérêts," "affaires") epitomizes a conventional metaphor that depends upon the possibility, repeatedly demonstrated in the *Maximes,* of representing the dynamics of egotism in economic terms. Describing a movement of intensifying externalization, from initial perception to calculative penetration, the series of verbs evokes the consciousness of self-love in pursuit of its principal interests: its attention, indivisible, is directed away from itself, toward objects accessible through direct perception. In the second part of the sentence, the conclusion drawn from this observation is stated with the greatest of reserve: "One is *tempted* to *believe.*" Believing is already one step removed from knowing; here there is only a temptation to believe, two steps removed from knowledge. Furthermore, the belief would concern an ill-defined property, a kind of magic that takes a particular form in each passion. As we have seen, the passions of self-love ("the diverse tastes of self-love," MP 28) are generated in its invisible depths, at a level where the force of instinctual drives excludes the presence of consciousness. Descending downward and inward from the level of an apprehending consciousness toward the directional center of self-love, one finds, then, in lieu of awakening self-awareness, a closing-off of consciousness and a consolidation of pure passion.

When the complex sentence is considered as a whole, the transition between the levels of conscious interest and unconscious passion appears to describe, at least nominally, a loose causal relationship (signaled by the subordinating conjunction "de sorte que") linking a statement about an observable (surface) activity to a potential explanation of it. This conception of cause on the basis of effect follows precisely the inferential process previously observed and thus displays a distinct sense of the tentative, exploratory character of that process. This kind of theoretical caution reappears shortly in the conditional and in the modalized adverb of the expression "whence one might conclude fairly reasonably," which governs a series of four possible conclusions. What remains nebulous, of course, is the magical transition whereby each passion can be said to acquire consciousness, then a measure of self-consciousness in its search for fulfillment. It is doubtless significant that the portrait of self-love fails to clarify this transition, which is subsumed in the process of personification. Before weighing the consequences of the limited awareness attributed to self-love, however, we should see whether the representation of the diverse passions in the *Maximes* provides deeper insight into the dynamics of wish-fulfillment.

As the portrait of self-love in MS 1 develops, it manifests a continuing effort to characterize the conduct of self-love by reference to the apparent objectives of its actions; but there is a change of emphasis insofar as the role of consciousness fades into the background and the impulsive character of affective life comes to the forefront. This shift of focus reproduces the predominant conjectural movement toward the core of self-love while putting greater stress on its internal energy and vitality:

Nothing is so strong and binding as its attachments, which it tries unsuccessfully to cast off in the face of the dire calamities that threaten it. Yet sometimes, quite rapidly and with no effort at all, does what it had been unable to do for many years. Whence one might conclude fairly reasonably that its desires are kindled by itself alone rather than by the beauty or value of the objects desired, which derive their worth and their luster from its taste, that self-love is running after itself, is doing what it likes in pursuing the things which are to its liking. . . . It is inconstant, and apart from changes due to outside causes there are countless others arising from within it, from its own resources. It is inconstant through sheer inconstancy, through shallowness, love, thirst for novelty, weariness, or disgust. It is capricious, and at times one sees it working with utmost eagerness and unbelievable toil to get things which are not at all advantageous to it, are sometimes even harmful, but which it pursues because it wants them.

At first glance, statements as elegantly pointed as these are in the original French seem to justify Moore's qualification of MS 1 as baroque in content but classical in style. Yet the undulatory movement of the lengthy sentences, relying heavily upon verbal and adverbial expressions of animation and rhetorical effects of antithesis, accumulation, resurgence, and focalization, makes this distinction somewhat dubious. Rather than from a tension or contradiction between style and content, the text derives its force from a significant correspondence or coordination between the dexterous manipulation of this admirably vibrant prose and the "travaux incroyables" that it evokes. For, as a verbal portrait, the text is distinguished by a telling concentration on dynamic traits: the representation of self-love in action takes complete precedence over the qualification of its being. Thus the descriptive style of MS 1, evocative rather than attributive, bears the mark of its elusive object; it connotes the impropriety of reducing self-love to a set of properties, of apprehending it as an essence.

While the description of incredible activity in the face of external influences upon action provides the observational context throughout the latter part of the reflection, the recurrent focal point of the discussion is the deep-seated, autonomous, self-motivating power of self-love: "*its* desires are kindled *by itself*"; "it is running *after itself*"; "it concentrates upon one ['se ramasse en une'] . . . as it pleases ['comme il lui plaît']"; "there are countless others *arising from within it, from its own resources*"; "which it pursues *because it wants them*"; "finally *it concerns itself only* with being." Whether set off by an opening disjunctive ("c'est . . . lui-même") or restrictive ("ne . . . que"), or underscored in its volitional or activational element at the end of a clause, the vital being of self-love is clearly removed from environmental dependence and credited with the self-sufficiency of being-in-itself. Self-love appears to be coming out of itself, moving after itself, and turning back into itself, acting as origin, object, and terminus, fusing being and desire in an irreducible life-instinct, a *vouloir-être* having no essence except metamorphosis, no principle or value dissociable from its perpetual release of energy. Beneath or beyond the stratum of being, there is no further state to evoke—save the extinction of being. While the scenario of its worldly intrigues could go on indefinitely, the portrait-in-depth of self-love has to stop at this point, where, as Bénichou notes, "the contours of the ego become blurred and disappear."[10]

By showing the interaction of self-love with "outside

10. Paul Bénichou, "L'Intention des *Maximes,*" *L'Ecrivain et ses trauvaux* (Paris, 1967), p. 10.

causes," MS 1 evinces the impossibility of a theory of self-love
that would provide a purely egotistical explanation of all human behavior. Through its speculative evocation of egocentricity, the text lays the groundwork for a less ambitious,
much less provocative theory, which postulates the action or
reaction of self-love in every human situation, but stops short
of "reducing man to a single feeling." It is, in fact, the complexity of self-love, mirroring but not duplicating the complexity of man, that the portrait brings into focus. In its central
thrust, this conjectural process aims, to be sure, to expose self-
love as a self-sufficient cause—"domestic" rather than foreign—
to show why many human actions may be directly equated with
those of self-love. The stress on its self-sufficiency can be understood in this light. Over against the contingency of appearances, the reality of self-love must be ongoing and self-per-
petuating if it is to explain appearances without reducing
everything, including itself, to irreality, in other words, without
promoting self-extinction. The fundamental demand upon a
theory of self-love is not simply that it delineate a being behind
the mask of appearances, but that it define a being that generates appearances, that it describe the motivation of appearances.

Clearly such a theory is limited by external constraints. The
pursuit of wish-fulfillment brings self-love into contact with
other causes, converts its action to interaction, bounds the sphere
of its autonomy. Moreover, in MS 1 self-love appears to act and
react as if it were aware of other principles and forces, as if
perceptions and value judgments, which, like some maxims,
recognize the limits of its power, can somehow be attributed to
it. Yet since the theory provides a uniform account of the aims
underlying individual action, it should be an extremely powerful one in providing for post facto explanation, even though, as
is still the case with theories of personality, it would be relatively weak (incapable of specificity) as a tool of prediction.

MS 1 does more than develop the traditional dichotomy of
being and appearance as a function of the equally common-

place spatial opposition between depth and surface. Complementing this scheme, by dint of an elaborate personification, the operation of a consciousness appears in conjunction with the rise of the passions toward external manifestation. The result is a rudimentary psychology that, since it can draw upon analogies with the operation of consciousness as it is ordinarily understood, has considerable utility as an instrument or framework for simplified, coherent representation of relatively complex phenomena. For the moralist, the subtle power of this instrument stems from its proximity to everyday experience: the reader's most "natural" associations incline him to assimilate his own thoughts and actions to those of self-love.

As long as the store of energy at the base of this hierarchical structure remains relatively stable, the theory of self-love should not only work, it should also undergo refinement and extension through repeated application. Here as elsewhere, the personification of self-love is of critical importance, for it is by acquiring consciousness—ultimately coincident with the consciousness of the individual—that self-love can embrace the whole of the world into which it projects itself. By the same token, this consciousness allows for the ready integration of all the *Maximes* into the theory of self-love. If self-love could not perceive obstacles, if it were not capable of the *calculated* pursuit of its interests (however ill conceived), the theory of self-love would be a trivial construct, subsumed by the facile assumption that egotistical motives always underlie human actions. Maxims that do not invoke such motives would appear unrelated to the theory, perhaps even contradictory. What vitalizes the theory is manifestly the bridge that it erects between desire and consciousness. The latter serves to open up the sphere of volitional activity and allows for the expansion of egotism into a veritable world-view. Within this enlarged theoretical framework, which, as MS 1 shows, corresponds to that of ordinary experience, no maxim can fall outside the purview of self-love. Maxims of a nonpsychological import serve to indicate the

boundaries of the theory, to clarify the relationship of desire to
other forms of causation.

The *Maximes* provide ample occasion for observing the conceptual utility of the theory of self-love. Functioning as a
hidden cause, self-love is readily available to provide a pre-
sumptive explanation for almost any kind of human conduct.
Overt evidence of this utility is provided by maxims that treat
actions as the inventions or effects of self-love: "The loyalty
visible in most men is merely a device invented by self-love in
order to attract confidence" (Max. 247; compare Max. 46, 83,
236, 494, MS 17, MP 33). The dependency of such explanations on a hidden cause, however, also embodies the major
theoretical problem besetting the notion of self-love. If the
Maximes pursue the elaboration of a theory of self-love, this
elaboration clearly takes place primarily in the sphere of effects,
at the surface level of conscious experience. Further penetration
into the unconscious functioning of desire is patently lacking. In
the portrait of self-love, the mystery of passion is protected by
the imagery of heavy shadows and a hovering night. The portrait associates the depth of being with darkness, with a cover
that obscures any cut-off point in the descent into self-love,
vaguely imagined as a bottomless abyss of instinctual energy.
The recourse to the naturally restricted language of obscurity
suggests that the core of being remains conceptually inaccessible:
"Whatever discoveries have been made in the land of self-love,
many of its regions remain unexplored" (Max. 3).

By now the use of the spatial metaphor to invoke the mysterious or unknown should not be unexpected. To represent self-
love as a land containing undiscovered (not merely unexplored)
regions is to deny the possibility of mapping its structure except
in an inadequate, fragmentary fashion. It is also to cut off the
deductive process, leading from surface to depth, which might
illuminate the vital link between conscious and unconscious
desire. In the final sentence of MS 1, a still more graphic
spatial image depicts the action, rather than the structure, of

self-love: "Such is the portrait of self-love, whose whole life is but a great, long agitation of which the sea is a tangible image. For in the ebb and flow of its unceasing waves self-love finds a faithful expression of the turbulent succession of its thoughts and its eternal movement."[11] As we noted in chapter 1, the image of the sea conveys both the variant movements of an ever-changing surface and the mystery of impenetrable depths. The geography of the sea becomes increasingly sketchy in areas where its bottom drops down into unchartable darkness. More persistently than the surface, it is the depth of experience that proves to be inconceivable and seems to suppress the work of the imagination. In the last analysis it is this internal elusiveness of self-love that works against the traditional understanding of its role in La Rochefoucauld's work.

An earlier comment on the halting evocation of the passions of self-love in MS 1 suggested that the theoretical consequences of this evasiveness would depend upon the degree to which understanding of the passions is developed in the *Maximes*. As is the case with self-love, the vast majority of maxims invoking the passions deal with their surface manifestations: "Whatever care one takes to veil his passions with appearances of piety and honor, they always show through" (Max. 12). And in the observation of the passions at work, just as with self-love, what is notable repeatedly turns out to be their imperious power to determine conduct: "All the passions cause us to make mistakes, but love causes us to make the most foolish ones" (Max. 422). With respect to the makeup of the passions in their deeper, more primitive state, the *Maximes* include little more than succinct confirmations of (or correspondences to) what is presented in MS 1. The following maxims evoke respectively the

11. This proposition presents in itself a rather succulent ambiguity: (1) self-love, whose entire life is made up solely of a long and massive agitation; (2) self-love, of which all (our) life is but a long and massive agitation. The second reading would correspond to the interpretation of the *Maximes* that sees in them a subordination of humanized life to the instinctual life of self-love. The context appears to require the first reading.

motifs of self-perpetuation, built-in contradiction, stimulation of consciousness and mystery:

In the human heart there is a perpetual generation of passions, such that the downfall of one is almost always the rise of another. [Max. 10]

Passions often engender their opposites. Avarice sometimes begets prodigality and prodigality avarice; man is often resolute through weakness, and bold through timidity. [Max. 11]

It seems that nature has hidden deep in our minds a skill and talents of which we are unaware; the passions alone are empowered to bring them to light, and sometimes to give us clearer and more finished insights than ingenuity could ever do. [Max. 404]

Comparing Maxim 404 to maxims dealing with the cleverness of self-love in order to shore up the distinction between these intertwined forces (one might say that self-love is a passion that encompasses the passions) reveals that consciousness is not directly attributed to passion, which, when personified, generally appears more violent and less wily than self-love.[12] Yet this very brutishness tends to steep passion more deeply in this dark reservoir of emerging energy, where only a quantitative representation of its nature seems possible: "All the passions are nothing else than the varying degrees of warmth, and of coldness, of the blood" (MS 2). If the type or quality of passion corresponds to the amount of energy expended, the mystery of the passions becomes the mystery of bodily process, ultimately, the mystery of life itself. At any rate, it is noteworthy that the recourse to a mechanistic explanation does not dissipate obscurity or substantiate knowledge in the *Maximes*— that, on the contrary, the handful of maxims reflecting a "materialist" outlook fit neatly into the category of demystifying statements that discredit conventional knowledge and ordinary

12. For something of an implicit attribution of consciousness to passion, see Max. 8 and 9.

conceptual patterns: "The bodily humors have their normal, appointed course which stirs and bends the will *imperceptibly;* they work in concert, and one by one exert a *secret* power within us, such that they play a considerable part in all of our actions, while *we are unable to be cognizant of them*" (Max. 297, italics added; compare Max. 44).

Thus the change of perspective from the psychological to the physical does not necessarily entail a significant clarification of the phenomena submerged within the self. It merely provides a simpler, more empirical amount of their manifestations. In the case of self-love and the passions, this account is clearly more consistent with the notion of nascent passion as a force or energy than the iconic version of MS 1. Yet the measurement of blood temperature would be a surface operation, no more apt to elucidate the generation of passions than the typology of various passionate conducts and less suited than the latter to the task of accounting for the human experience of passion in its integrality. In maxims dealing with particular passions such as love and envy, surface manifestations also predominate, also leave the obscurity at the heart of MS 1 intact. Thus the fleeting underpinnings of the passions, like those of self-love, tend to undercut the systematic application of a psychic determinism.

Although the obscure relationship of desire to consciousness constitutes a serious problem within the portrait of self-love, in no sense does it detract from the seriousness of the text. Under the pressure of analysis, the portrait proves to be a surprisingly measured statement. We have already noted some remarkable expressions of intellectual reservations tempering the confident tone of the text as it moves away from axiomatic affirmations toward tentative insights into the depths of passion, eventually unveiling the extent to which self-love remains inaccessible to nonmetaphorical understanding. Indeed, what the text lacks is not so much logical consistency as full imaginative development. Moreover, although MS 1 turns out to be relatively unpretentious, at least in comparison to many maxims, it is nevertheless a self-conscious text. Not merely is its rhetoric transparent (the last sentence actually declares that the image of the sea is appropriate), but it insists on the difficulties of perception and representation, and its stress on the problematical nature of egological phenomena constitutes a certain internal justification for resorting to stylistic bravura. In other words, the text unmistakably evinces its "literarity" and proceeds to justify it. The gist of its statement, abstracted from the rhetoric, lays the foundation for a dispassionate psychological theory and deserves to be taken at face value.

Critics have squandered valuable time trying to decide whether the *Maximes* represent the application or elaboration of a system. Although this now seems to be a marginal issue outside the sphere of ethical questions, it is perhaps pertinent to recognize at this point that the *Maximes,* grounded in a hypothetical view of self-love, revealing its underlying fugacity, hardly deserve to be portrayed as the inflexible organ of a "system of self-love." The more vital issue relating to self-love concerns the consequences of this internal fugacity: does it dislodge self-love from the central position in the work that tradition accords it and disable the theory of self-love that the foregoing analysis purports to sustain?

Self-love is no less central for being thrown into question. The problematical nature of its underpinnings clearly adds an important limitation to the theory, which is, in effect, bounded by its own, self-centering constraints as well as by external forces of causation. The postulate situating an incredible mystery at the heart of self-love jeopardizes the process of verification and fixes the theory at the stage of the hypothetical. Yet because the concept of self-love functions as a potent reductive force in maxims dealing with morality, there is nevertheless a temptation to attribute to the *Maximes* a much more doctrinaire theory of self-love than the one which the work allows. If, from a purely moral standpoint, self-love is treated as nothing more than a system of egotistic exploitation, the relationship between the scheming activity depicted in the first part of MS 1 and the capricious "essence" toward which the portrait evolves becomes an intractable contradiction. Insofar as the flow of appetitive energy defies moral qualification and enters into a natural association with a promiscuous physical determinism, the notion of moral responsibility, and with it the denunciation of egotism, may be summarily invalidated.

As we noted earlier, the interpretation and/or conciliation of these conflicting methods of explanation—"the system of self-love and the idea of an indifferent and capricious causality governing man"[13]—have preoccupied recent critics of the *Maximes,* who appear to vacillate between two basic outlooks. Nowhere is this opposition more transparent than in the portrait of self-love; and to the extent that MS 1 serves as the introductory cornerstone of the *Maximes,* it should allow us to delineate the psychological context in which the problem of moral responsibility arises. The clearest and most rigorous exposition and elucidation of the problem appears in the study of the *Maximes* by Paul Bénichou, who specifies the critical assumption that comes into play:

The denunciation of self-love entails an implicit blaming: what is discovered in man is base, detestable; odious. . . . This indictment of good conscience naturally supposes a psychology of the unconscious. . . . But it is necessary to note that what is of a psychological order in his analyses, namely the distinction, for a given action, of a motive formulated by the consciousness of the subject and a secret motive, entirely different, supposes a pre-existing moral order.[14]

The assumption is that La Rochefoucauld invents a psychology of self-love as a function of a fundamentally moralistic outlook, that the motivation of his psychological insights is inferentially that of moral condemnation.

13. Bénichou, *L'Ecrivain,* p. 9.
14. Ibid., pp. 5–6.

Even if the often vilified MS 1 is considered representative of La Rochefoucauld's activity as a moralist, there is serious cause to question this assumption. Only at the beginning does the portrait contain so much as a hint of moral imputation, which is at least implicit in the declaration that self-love "makes men *worshipers* of themselves, and would make them *tyrants* over others, if fortune gave them the means" (italics added). Just as the pejorative note transmitted by *idolâtre* and *tyrans* is undeniable, so is the explanatory value of the statement manifest. The action of self-love as a determinative factor clearly overrides any moral objection that might be consciously opposed to it. Bénichou is entirely correct in affirming that the qualification of hidden motives (that is, real as opposed to avowed) often incorporates the assumptions of conventional moral judgment. This, however, means simply that the moral judgment has preceded the formulation of the distinction between conscious and secret motives and that it bears upon the profession of false, superficial motives. Clearly it cannot mean that moral judgment presupposes absolute freedom to opt for unimpeachable action. On the contrary, the psychic impulse to wish-fulfillment necessarily precedes the conception of moral conduct, for the latter is meaningful only by virtue of an originary opposition to amoral instinct.

At any rate, the presentation of self-love at the outset of MS 1 suggests that egotism is an independent force of such might that nothing can overcome its motivational predominance, hence that man's prerogative to pass negative judgment on various actions attributable to self-love in no way entails his full moral responsibility for those actions. In other words, whether their manifestations are obvious or sheltered, the drives of self-love inevitably tend to exculpate man insofar as his actions in themselves are concerned. But this exculpation is incomplete and ambiguous. Once again the origin of difficulty lies in the elusive connection of desire and consciousness in self-love. In this case, moreover, the connection is made all the more problematical because self-love achieves only distorted self-perception, because its self-awareness is always self-deceptive. What is left in limbo, then, is the capacity of consciousness to direct and control the energy that drives it. Or, in other terms, what the portrait of self-love leaves undetermined is the extent to which the consciousness attributed to self-love can be considered willfully malignant.

What is clear is that the moral judgments of the *Maximes* can lay only claim to a limited scope of validity and that they will have to qualify, above all, the exercise of consciousness. Since it is precisely by managing to pass unrecognized or misunderstood that the activity of self-love can relegate man to amoral dependency, the attempt to advance psychological understanding by spying out self-love serves as a necessary first step toward instituting the possibility of a meaningful ethic. Logically, the moral is not prior to the psychological. By virtue of their dispassionate tone as well as their introspective content, maxims that purport to denounce—that is, to unveil—self-love qualify as bona fide statements of a psychological order. The moral accusation implicit in them is directed at the victim's failure to understand or represent his actions correctly, at his tacit complicity with the malfunctioning self-consciousness of self-love. Before we can appraise the axiology of the *Maximes,* we have to take measure of the psychology underlying it.

In La Rochefoucauld's self-portrait, which antedates the *Maximes* and the *Réflexions,* a stylized approach to the problem of self-representation associates the development of psychological insight with the practice of introspection, invoked with an accent akin to that of Montaigne: "I have studied myself enough to know myself well, and I am not lacking either in the self-assurance to state openly such good qualities as I may have, or in the sincerity to admit frankly to my faults."[15] As a kind of

15. See the Truchet edition, pp. 251–58, for the self-portrait. This citation, p. 252.

psychological prelude to the *Maximes,* this self-analysis fore-
shadows a representation of the human personality that requires a modest apparatus of psychological categories. Predict-
ably enough, the intimation of a fairly methodical introspection
gives rise to a critical hypothesis according to which La Rochefoucauld's psychology corresponds to the makeup of his own
personality. This gives rise in turn to a potential confusion between the results of a psychologically oriented attempt to understand the character of La Rochefoucauld and the results of La
Rochefoucauld's own ventures into the area of psychology. In
short, analyzing the personality of La Rochefoucauld would
mean dissecting his psychology and his psyche in the same
breath.[16]

This dual approach to La Rochefoucauld's psychology can,
of course, be carried on at more than one level. As a matter of
circumstance, there is a tendency to read La Rochefoucauld's
self-portrait in conjunction with the portrait of La Rochefoucauld by the Cardinal de Retz. The latter document challenges
La Rochefoucauld's claim to self-knowledge while putting the
accent on the mysteries of La Rochefoucauld's conduct: "There
has always been something enigmatic in everything having to
do with M. de la Rochefoucauld. . . . He has always been
chronically irresolute, but I cannot even explain this irresolution. . . . We see the effects of this irresolution although we
do not know its cause. . . . He would have done much better
to learn to know himself and to confine himself to playing the
part, as he could have done, of the most accomplished courtier
of his age."[17]

Through his portrait, which concentrates on La Rochefoucauld's appearance, actions, and the type of perception and
thinking that they reflect, Retz points by implication to the
necessity of a deeper understanding of La Rochefoucauld's con-

16. Mora, *François de La Rochefoucauld,* p. 58, for instance: "This
work . . . is intimately at one with the author's life and his whole personality—including even his subconscious *ego.*"
17. Quoted in the Truchet edition, p. 58, note.

flicting motivations, one not within the province of his own extrinsic, somewhat slanted observation. Subsequent attempts to extend comprehension of La Rochefoucauld's personality invariably set out to elucidate the "something enigmatic" and the "chronic irresolution" to which Retz alludes. The standard insight remains that of Saint-Beuve, who speculated that the duke's irresolute character grew out of his intellectual acuity, his skeptical, ironic mode of perception, which always saw through a strategic situation too well, anticipating and thereby abetting the ineffectiveness of action.[18] To some extent, the *Mémoires* of La Rochefoucauld support this view, although the author is wont to insist upon his propensity to take decisive action despite his private scruples.

Regardless of the accuracy of Sainte-Beuve's model explanation, by tying behavior to the exercise of conscious reflection it achieves little or no significant psychological penetration. The considerable difficulty of such penetration comes to light within La Rochefoucauld's self-portrait in two ways. First, he fails to elaborate extensively upon the nature of his inner self, which he appears to introduce as the logical complement of his physical appearance. Second, he admits to being very reserved and secretive. We can, nonetheless, glean from his explanations of character and conduct a number of factors outside the purview of immediate consciousness:

To speak first about my disposition, I am melancholic, and to such a degree that I have scarcely been seen to laugh more than three or four times in the last three or four years. Still, my melancholy would be fairly mild and tolerable, I believe, if I had only that melancholy which comes from my temperament; but I have so much coming from elsewhere, the effect of which is to fill my imagination and to occupy my mind to such an extent that most of the time either I am dreaming while saying not a word or I have almost no control over what I am saying. . . . So once again, I am intelligent, but melan-

18. Sainte-Beuve, "M. de La Rochefoucauld," *Portraits de femmes* (Paris, 1862), pp. 260–63.

choly spoils my intelligence; for, while I have good control of my
tongue, and have an accurate memory, and am not given to muddled
thinking, I am so immersed in my despondency that I often express
quite poorly what I mean to say.[19]

This text turns upon two versions of the same causal relationship: melancholy temperament produces a discontinuity of
thought and speech, or, more precisely, the mental inflection of
temperament introduces a division within thought itself, conceived as a space that is *occupied* or *filled* by the invading
sources of discontent. Thus the thought actually enunciated incorporates only a fraction of a complete intellection, fails to
reflect the full control of a unified, self-directed mind. If La
Rochefoucauld's character is to be explained by the quality of
his thinking, it would, then, depend upon an element of disen-
gagement or distraction within the act of reflection.

Yet the portrait clearly relates this interference with reflection to extramental phenomena, originating in the temperament
or elsewhere, and thereby introduces a properly psychological
perspective, which posits dynamic interrelations between the
levels of the self and between the whole self and its environment. As Starobinski emphasizes, however, the other influences—allusively invoked by the phrase *tant d'ailleurs*—go
unnamed, remaining open to speculation.[20] Instead of pursuing
the path of psychological elucidation, La Rochefoucauld turns
to his views on coexistence with other people and thereafter
refers to his feelings and passions only in this *sociological* context. Hastily conceding that his reluctance to enter into confi-
dential relationships is a fault that he would like to correct, he
immediately proceeds to link his reticence to a principle of
social discretion, not only defending his stance as a contribution
to interpersonal harmony, but justifying it initially on the basis
of a generic inability to correlate an internal correction with
visible demeanor: "But as a certain morosity in my facial ex-

19. Truchet edition, p. 254.
20. Introduction, p. 32.

pression tends to make me look even more reserved than I am, and since it is not in our power to rid ourselves of a malevolent expression which originates in the natural arrangement of our features, I think that after having corrected myself internally, I shall still bear these unfortunate markings externally."[21]

One might suppose that, for La Rochefoucauld, this self-correction would mean attaining a more confident self-expression by unifying his previously divided thought so as to concentrate completely upon the matter of his discourse. Were this accomplished, however, the natural disposition of physical features would still interfere with the communication of the change in mental disposition, which cannot be proved to others by words alone. As the sharply drawn distinction between the inside and the outside picks up the opposition of the mental and the physical, it becomes clear that the chief obstacle to the integration of personality arises from the natural disjunction of being and appearance. The nonconformity of appearance to being does not originate in the invention of disguise; it lies in the very fabric of the human condition, in the limited power of mind over matter, which constrains the former to develop a strategy with respect to the latter.

Far from constituting a *real* flaw in his character, La Rochefoucauld's reserve reflects his sensitivity to the difficulty of maintaining a maximum of control over the interpretation of one's external appearance. Indeed, the entire self-portrait can be read in this light as an attempt to limit and to orient the perception of its readers, to sidestep the troubling lessons of introspection that La Rochefoucauld is on the verge of broaching. "What La Rochefoucauld's portrait reveals to us is the refusal to expose himself and to reveal himself 'in depth'—and perhaps the refusal to attribute an exceptional value to this hidden depth. . . . As an *honnête homme* the Duke of La Rochefoucauld, so interested in analyzing the causes which motivate men, so anxious to be a party to the 'secrets of the kingdom,' succeeds in keeping

21. Truchet edition, p. 254.

secret the causes (if there are causes) which determine his own conduct."[22]

Starobinski goes on to stress the element of convention in La Rochefoucauld's melancholy (other self-portraits in the *Galerie de Mlle de Montpensier* lay claim to the same "aristocratic affection") and in the conception of the self-portrait itself. Its deference to the protocol of genteel society takes La Rochefoucauld's self-portrait to the opposite pole from Montaigne's forthright self-portrayal, leaving the deeper exploration of the self to a nonconfessional, impersonal mode of expression. The particular psychological interest of the portrait centers less on the personality of La Rochefoucauld than on the underlying model of the *honnête homme* to which both the genre and the author's image of himself are subservient: "I hold virtuous opinions, have noble instincts and such a strong desire to be a thoroughgoing *honnête homme* that my friends could give me no greater pleasure than to inform me sincerely of my shortcomings."[23] At this level of discourse, where penetration into the private self is held back by the quality of perception and by the prevailing values of one's peers, La Rochefoucauld forces his reader to confront the impossibility of directly acceding to a psychological explanation of his thought and action.

What lesson should be drawn from La Rochefoucauld's abstention from diagnostic self-disclosure? Does his confessional silence conceal an untouchable secret that we should seek to penetrate in analyzing his work? In their concerted impersonality, the *Maximes* leave no doubt that, in lieu of an introspective approach, La Rochefoucauld centers the formulation, if not the conception, of his psychology upon the behavior of others. To some extent, the theory of self-love requires this approach, for it grants the possibility of acute external perception while affirming the impossibility of accurate self-perception.

22. Starobinski, introduction, p. 32.
23. Truchet edition, p. 256.

To seek self-understanding is to apply to oneself the lessons derived from observing others. In any case, the *Maximes* and the *Réflexions* record perceptions that are represented as perceptions of others; and since these perceptions are merged into the image of a composite being, universal Man, the books seem to be studiously depersonalized, highly resistant to psychoanalytic probes in the direction of their distant author. In addition, La Rochefoucauld's writing is dominated by a limited number of patently standard themes, and it is generally felt that the stylist's persistence in honing and polishing the *Maximes* tends to diminish still further the incidence of telltale clues to the author's complexes, obsessions, or unconscious intentions. The effacement of authorial presence has motivated two important interpretations, that of Barthes, who elects to treat La Rochefoucauld's main themes as obsessions, and that of Jeanson, who views La Rochefoucauld's concentration upon the behavior of other men as a case of Sartrean bad faith.

In affirming that the *Maximes,* because they turn incessantly on the themes of love, passion, and virtue, are an obsessional work, Barthes immediately responds to the objection that these are simply the great themes of La Rochefoucauld's time, upon which he naturally focused his attention: "But La Rochefoucauld always says the same thing about them; the insistence, for example, with which he comes back to self-love, the eloquence which seems to seize him on the subject, and especially the very dialectic of the obsession, which allows for varying the point of view while holding on to the mania for the theme, all this seems to reveal a veritable alienation of the author from his subject. . . . A maxim is something of a rut, the deep trace of a mind's reversions to a single subject."[24] Thus the writing of maxims would require not so much the writer's interest in certain subjects as his subjection to his subject, and the stylistic refinement of the maxim would represent, rather than a suppression or concealment of obsessions, a movement toward their

24. Introduction, p. xxxvii.

barren exposure. "The maxim speaks La Rochefoucauld, perhaps less what he would wish to think than what he cannot
keep from thinking."[25]

In regard to the subject of virtue, for example, Barthes suggests that the thematic importance of a given virtue depends
upon the degree to which the practice of that virtue is obsessive
for La Rochefoucauld. He adds, moreover, that the strength of
the obsession correlates with the depth of illusion incorporated
in the accompanying state of good conscience. To the obsession
with basic themes corresponds an obsession with a basic form,
the root structure of the maxim, so that Barthes, although he
fails to develop extensively this idea of a formal obsession,
would presumably admit that there is likewise an alienation of
the author from his mode of expression, visible in La Rochefoucauld's willingness to subject the message of the maxim to
"the distance of the aphorism."[26]

Barthes's argument does not afford him any explicit insight
into the genesis of such a dual alienation (with respect to
theme and to form), but the coupling of alienation to a closed
obsessional dialectic that allows only variations on its basic
thematics and form clearly suggests that the impersonality and
uniformity of La Rochefoucauld's writing, along with his re-
iterative debunking of man in general, must be related to the
insuperable interdictions of a stultifying environment. La Rochefoucauld would have fixed upon his themes in a defensive
response to an alien world insensitive to his private truth. What
determines—or becomes—the object of interpretation is precisely La Rochefoucauld's refusal to accredit introspection or
individuality, confirmed in the concentration of his writings
on interpersonal relations. Indeed, the analyst who seeks to
recapture this supremely absent author within his work has no
alternative to following the lead of La Rochefoucauld's self-
portrait, where the emphasis shifts from the psychological toward the sociological. Within the *Maximes* and the *Réflexions*,

25. Ibid., p. lxxvi.
26. Ibid., pp. lxxvi–lxxvii.

the main clues to the dynamics of this shift have to be garnered from the representations of social phenomena.

In recasting his analysis in a sociohistorical context, Barthes sets up a neat conceptual framework within which he can link the alienation of the individual to that of his group. For the individual (La Rochefoucauld) the maxim, in the process of expressing his alienation from certain constituents of a moral outlook, also liberates him from them, thus fulfilling a cathartic function no less effectively than free expression on an analyst's couch. For the group, collectively haunted by the same obsessional themes as La Rochefoucauld, the *Maximes* would also have a liberating function, drawing out the previously repressed truth of illusion. As the dialectic of La Rochefoucauld's obsessions merges with that of the group's obsessions, it becomes clear that Barthes's scheme affords little credence to the notion that La Rochefoucauld's psychology coincides with an introspective view of the personality or represents the exercise of the individual's intellectual curiosity about himself or his attempt to deal objectively with his private neuroses. Instead, the elaboration of a psychology in the *Maximes* would reflect, in its inception and construction, the irresistible pressure of external stimuli and would be oriented less around the personality of the individual than around the mentality characteristic of his caste.

Jeanson's attack on La Rochefoucauld appears to radicalize the basic assumption of Barthes's analysis. Whereas the latter supposes that, fundamentally, La Rochefoucauld is obsessed with the society of peers from which he is alienated, Jeanson takes the moralist to be obsessed with establishing his own superiority to other people. The outward orientation of La Rochefoucauld's psychology does not, therefore, simply reveal his private obsession; it offers a primary illustration of Jeanson's general thesis according to which La Rochefoucauld's entire intellectual enterprise is governed by his desire to guarantee his own superiority. The moralist tries to maintain his position of authority by doing nothing more than exposing the subservience of others; he attempts to *be* a superior man without having to *become* one. Jeanson argues that La Rochefoucauld could retain contradictory explanations of conduct because each explanation would serve his ultimate goal: "It is just a matter of reducing human activities to infrahuman elements, escaping from the control and initiative of man."[27] As the lucid analyst of human nature, La Rochefoucauld would have definitively transcended his own nature, understanding it as an externalized object and repossessing it, through a kind of esthetic purification, as a unique, original work of art.

Thus the moralist invents his psychology strictly in order to escape from its sphere of validity, and if he infuses it with a high valuation of sincerity, he does so only in order to dispense with the challenge that other men—condemned to lowly falsehood—might pose to his superiority, in order to gain credibility for his own claim to be innately unique and ineffable: "The whole of La Rochefoucauld's psychology is thus grounded on the split between a being-for-itself which is totally determined, and a being-for-others which is fully defined by the concern with appearance";[28] La Rochefoucauld manages to advocate an undivided concern with one's own *être-pour-soi* while passively satisfying, by means of his supposedly absolute sincerity, the discarded concern with appearances. This sincerity, masking the inescapable concern for others, is only a lie of consciousness to itself about itself—or bad faith. Thus Jeanson dismisses La Rochefoucauld's belittlement of man as a false psychology, within which the moralist's superficial understanding of his consciousness constitutes a self-serving prelude for his constant preoccupation with the all-too-human nature of others. Owing to this preoccupation, La Rochefoucauld's psychology can obtain only a very limited sphere of validity: it may account for a given instance of human conduct, but it cannot do justice to the totality of man's existence.

Jeanson's existentialist analysis is hardly compatible with the Marxist-Freudian views implicit in Barthes's interpretation;

27. *Lignes de départ,* p. 80.
28. Ibid., p. 87.

similarly, the latter's concern with elucidating a writer's outlook stops well short of Jeanson's aggressively moralistic denunciation. Yet their respective conclusions conform insofar as they undercut the intellectual integrity of La Rochefoucauld's psychology and severely restrict its validity. In order to penetrate the character of La Rochefoucauld through his psychology, each critic turns his attention away from the structure and import of the psychology in question and concentrates upon the motivation(s) behind its creation or orientation. Where Bénichou perceives, beneath the psychology of the unconscious, a concern with moral judgment, Barthes and Jeanson go on to point, in psychological terms, to a more deeply personal obsession or complex. As a function of this unconscious or repressed factor, the psychology of self-love would serve variously as a defense mechanism (against the encroachment of desire upon the moralist's image of himself) or as a protective shield (against the deflation of that self-image by others). Such an explanation makes the status of that psychology contingent upon psychological factors that its own superstructure fails to encompass, and its values are inevitably subordinated to those of the critic's analytical position.

This is particularly blatant in Jeanson's unsympathetic treatment, where the restriction of La Rochefoucauld's psychology to a narrow sphere of applicability is grounded in an activist notion of a man's existence—"man is ceaselessly exposed; he 'is' only by his actions"[29]—which goes beyond the conceptual patterns of the seventeenth-century moralist. If we choose to question its motivations, we can restrict the value of Jeanson's critical analysis in a similar way. Setting forth La Rochefoucauld's position in conjunction with a psychoanalytic approach to his world-view almost inevitably leads to representing his psychology in terms of—and thus in inferior relation to—the presumably more powerful psychology that informs the analysis. This approach tends therefore to preclude a thorough examination of La Rochefoucauld's psychology in itself and in relation

29. Ibid., p. 89.

to the works within which it is developed. To do justice to these works, in their detachment from authorial presence, it is necessary to delineate methodically the structure of that psychology and to see how it works without regard for the motivations that underlie it.

While La Rochefoucauld's psychology has always been closely identified with the theory of self-love, its logical starting point lies in the view of the personality that is at the basis of the self-portrait. As we have noted, this "secretive" text does rely upon a loose conceptual apparatus into which the balance of La Rochefoucauld's psychological vocabulary can be fitted. Although the basic terminological distinctions tend to cloud up as more refined relationships are introduced, it seems appropriate to begin with a rough schematic representation of the categories employed in this verbal portrait of the personality. The primary categories are those of being (*le dedans*), as opposed to appearance, and they fall naturally into a vertical configuration that descends from the purely mental toward the emotional and physical. Adjacent to them, we note some examples of manifestations or appearances that, in the portrait, correspond to these functions of personality.

IMAGINATION   talents d'érivain

ESPRIT: connaissance
   (conscience)
   Raison   critique, délicatesse, plaisirs et satisfaction
   Jugement   dans la conversation, civilité
   Mémoire
   Goût

COEUR — AME[30]
   Passions   ambition, pitié, courage, belles passions,
   Inclinations   bonnes inclinations, austère vertu, sévère

---

30. This dubious correspondence of heart to soul occurs here only because this preliminary sketch is based exclusively upon the self-portrait, in which the lone reference to the soul concerns "la grandeur de l'âme," which is associated with "les belles passions."

Sentiments	sagesse, parole régulière
Envie	
Devoir	

TEMPERAMENT

| Humeur | mélancolie, chagrin |

| CORPS: la disposition | air sombre, tout le portrait physique |
| naturelle des traits | |

Through its emphatic distinction of *qualités* and *défauts* and an equally sharp awareness of excess and deficiency, the self-portrait shows that each element in this provisional tableau of the personality is subject to moral and/or esthetic qualification. Just as the axiological autonomy of the mind seems indubitable, it is clear that the interplay among the various strata of the personality entails a thoroughgoing interdependence. It is equally clear that grasping the dynamics of this interdependence constitutes a crucial psychological problem for La Rochefoucauld. Yet the portraitist's practice of desisting from anything more than the sketchiest of hints on the interrelations within the self is poignantly illustrated at the close of his text. La Rochefoucauld's ultimate avowal that he would be unlikely to traverse the gulf between the mental understanding of love and the emotional experience of love stands as a symptomatic enigma: "But being made as I am, I do not think that this knowledge of mine will ever pass from my mind to my heart." Pithy and pointed as a maxim, this curiously phrased pseudo-confession is couched in a semantic ambivalence that stands as a final reminder of the writer's elusiveness: in terms of the portrait's insistence on psychological inadequacy, we may understand that the knowledge of love is confined to the mind, incommunicable, and of no use to the heart; yet, in terms of an ironic viewpoint on love, we may read this same admission as the cynic's suggestion that experience with love has taught him the folly of engaging in it, of taking his knowledge of love to heart. In either case, the dominant motif is the *separation* of

knowledge from action or emotion. The writer's secret in his
self-portrait consists precisely in the silence that he maintains
with respect to the channels connecting the mind to the heart;
as in the portrait of self-love, he evokes a logic of the self
without unveiling its operational principles.

To some extent, the structure outlined on the basis of the
portrait can be filled in through reference to La Rochefoucauld's
other works, where the general pattern for conceiving of the
personality remains the same. Diagraming the self-portrait's
psychological vocabulary reveals one glaring omission—self-
love—by which the professed disjunction of thought and speech
might well have been explained. In addition to the concept of
self-love, the *Maximes* and certain *Réflexions* make use of a
rudimentary medical terminology (*santé, maladie, guérison,
remède,* and so forth) which can be applied within this conceptual framework. Taking into account the wide range of
meaning covered by such terms as self-love and soul, we are
obliged to recognize that the stratified view of the self remains
tacit and very approximate and does not suppress the confusion
prevailing within the active personality. A simplified view of
the major categories illustrates the prominence of interconnec-
tion, merging, and overlapping that characterize the actual
functioning of this psychology:

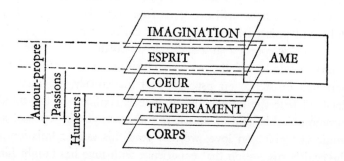

This graphic representation hardly suggests a very technical
perspective. Aside from the lack of clear-cut separations between the strata, more properly analogous to intermingling

levels of soil than to rungs of a ladder, the predominant feature
of the diagram is clearly the mobility and transmutability of
energy, exemplified by the multilevel assertions of self-love.
Since the various categories and psychophysical forces are conventional in conception, it is only by magnifying their aptitude
for interaction that La Rochefoucauld can invigorate the limited
terminology at his disposal. *Grosso modo*, pursuing psychological insights may involve either of two processes: pinpointing
the sources and manifestations of psychic energy or developing
variations on elementary distinctions between the levels of the
self—*esprit/coeur, esprit/corps, âme/corps*. While the outlines
of a commonsensical system inevitably inform this undertaking,
it is not a question of constructing a tightly knit system through
precise definitions and delimitations, but of manipulating the
resources of an inherited terminology, characterized by loose
notions rather than rigid concepts.

The nature of psychological understanding in the *Maximes*
comes to light in the relations between the mental and the
physical: "The health of the *soul* is no more stable than that of
the *body;* and though we may seem to stand aloof from the
passions we are just as liable to be carried away by them as to
fall ill when in good health" (Max. 188). A comparable
distinction prevails between the mind and the heart (a center of
passions, see Max. 10): "Man often believes he is in control
while he is being controlled; and while his *mind* is striving in
one direction, his *heart* is drawing him imperceptibly in another"
(Max. 43). Maxim 188 implicitly defines good mental health
as a state in which the passions, like infectious germs, are held
in check, in which the soul maintains its presence of mind in
the face of an internal menace. The analogy between the soul
and the body is pertinent precisely because each falls ill in the
same way, without warning, a prey to the insidious outbreak of
disease. While the effects of compelling passion are, if imperious, at least identifiable, the stealthier movements of the heart
and the body quietly subvert man's conscious designs, threaten-
ing the presumed status of the mind not so much by escaping

from its control as by acting secretly, by escaping from its perception and compromising man's self-understanding.

The overall thrust of this psychology centers, then, on the incompetence of man's mental resources in dealing with physical and emotional drives. We have already cited one text (Max. 297) in which the invocation of the theory of humors, secretively undermining man's pretensions to will power, carries strong deterministic implications. The subtle influence of the heart is no less constant than that of the humors: "The mind is always fooled by the heart" (Max. 102). Pointing to the imperceptible secret power of the humors parallels the disclosure of the heart's covert influence in that both underlie the deception of the mind. To the elucidation of this deception La Rochefoucauld's psychology is largely devoted. And as the analysis of self-love suggests, the fundamental problem disclosed by this focus concerns man's potential for self-disabusal, the means by which and extent to which the mind can counter the forces of illusion. Those who confine La Rochefoucauld's representation of the human condition to the psychology of self-love, of love, or of passion concentrate unduly upon what La Rochefoucauld takes to be given patterns of human conduct instead of emphasizing the mental phenomena he seeks to divulge and explain. It would be more appropriate to speak of a psychology of deficient consciousness, while noting, as does Paul Masson-Oursel, that his psychology—in its course of elaboration—more nearly approximates a phenomenology.[31]

If the *Maximes* have been appreciated traditionally for their psychological penetration, they have not maintained this reputation by any rigorously scientific standard. As frequently occurs with authors of the so-called psychological novel, in speaking of La Rochefoucauld's psychological acumen or his "knowledge of the human heart," one refers in fact to a nontechnical viewpoint, characterized by incisive representations of the motivations of behavior. However systematic they may look in

31. "La Rochefoucauld devant l'inconscient," *Psyché*, II, 4 (1947), 143–49.

combination, each of the artist's particular perceptions initially belongs to the subjective sphere of intuition or suspicion, rather than to ordered speculation or experimental observation. If the moralist's art accentuates the movement of intellection, it does not reflect the methodological distance of scientific writing; it retains the imprint of spontaneous insight, reflects the close, yet unexplained connection of thought to feeling, of judgment to taste, and of mind to heart.

In the particular case of La Rochefoucauld, what is inevitably perceived as authentically psychological is nothing other than the imagination of unconscious existence. "La Rochefoucauld is one of the first to have utilized, without naming it, the unconscious: for him, self-love *hides* itself in a great variety of forms. . . . In a general way it has subsequently been recognized that, if the ego is not present to consciousness, it is hidden behind it and is the magnetic center of all our representations and all our wishes."[32] It should be noted that in La Rochefoucauld, no less than in the work of contemporary psychology, the territory of the unconscious remains large and imprecisely delineated and encompasses impulses emanating from the Freudian id and superego as well as the ego. The wide range of self-love's activity precludes reducing unconscious activity to that of a submerged ego. That La Rochefoucauld does not have at his command an explicit concept of the unconscious confers upon his thinking a significant limitation that Sartre ignores: the inability to represent unconscious existence as such, as a separate scene of action, in full dissociation from consciousness.

In his critique, Sartre seeks to demonstrate that a notion of the unconscious is useless and erroneous because it stems from an incomplete understanding of consciousness, grasped only in its reflexive or thetic structure. The crux of his objection to La Rochefoucauld's psychology bears upon the illogicality of envisaging reflexive activity in the unconscious—carried out, according to Sartre, so as to bestow upon nonthetic acts the

32. Jean-Paul Sartre, *La Transcendance de l'ego* (Paris, 1966), p. 38.

structure of reflexive acts. Thus, for example, the "moraliste de l'amour-propre" would suppose that, within the spontaneous act of pity and assistance for a wounded person, an unconscious agent of the self is actually prompting the actor to identify himself with benevolent conduct—is substituting, in effect, for the reflexive consciousness that would recognize this act as *his* benevolence, which he should pursue as *his* duty. Insisting upon the real spontaneity of such actions, Sartre argues that egotistic activity occurs only on the level of reflection, that desire is originally pure and is contaminated when perceived as one's own desire, to be cultivated as one's property. "Before being poisoned my wishes were pure; it is the point of view that I have adopted toward them, which has poisoned them. La Rochefoucauld's psychology is true only for the particular feelings which have their origin in reflective activity, that is, which are grasped initially as *my feelings,* instead of first moving beyond themselves toward an object."[33] In other words, by denying that egocentricity can prevail unconsciously, outside the sphere of a reflecting ego, Sartre claims to invalidate the most consequential part of La Rochefoucauld's psychology, that which links behavior to a uniform motivational structure.

Although the psychological viewpoint developed in Sartre's early work has been largely eclipsed by his later writings, his provocative view of the "theoreticians of self-love" does force us to look closely at the use La Rochefoucauld makes of the unconscious. Sartre's critique clearly does not pertain directly to all unconscious life; it applies specifically to that unconscious which consists of a submerged consciousness, operating outside the purview of ordinary perception. Thus Sartre challenges essentially the personification of instinctive self-love—and by extension the personification of secretive passions such as sloth. If, on occasion, La Rochefoucauld brings out an unconscious conditioning of behavior that is rooted strictly in *physiological* factors, the validity of his insights would be challenged by

33. Ibid., p. 40.

Sartre only insofar as they might be used to absolve the consciousness of responsibility for its acts.

Now, in the *Maximes* and the *Réflexions* the incidence of recourse to some form of submerged consciousness is relatively low. In most cases, the activity of self-love and its conscious agent, interest, clearly presupposes the activity of a reflecting ego, which La Rochefoucauld takes to task primarily because of its apparent inattention to its egocentric nature. On this level, ordinary consciousness and the consciousness of self-love appear to coincide. Only rarely does the type of spontaneous, uncalculated reaction upon which Sartre insists come into question. There are, however, in addition to the conspicuous example of MS 1, enough instances of a submerged or repressed consciousness to confirm its status as a necessary conceptual tool in La Rochefoucauld's attempt to account for human behavior:

It seems that self-love is tricked by benevolence, and that it forgets itself when we work for the benefit of others. Yet this is its surest way to achieve its goals; it is lending at interest while pretending to give, is ultimately a subtle and delicate means of acquiring favor from everyone. [Max. 236]

Our first impulse of joy at the good fortune of our friends comes neither from our natural benevolence, nor from our affection for them; it is an effect of self-love, which charms us with the hope that we may in turn be lucky or else derive some benefit from their good fortune. [MS 17]

These maxims clearly represent the type of understanding to which Sartre objects. The first evokes the image of self-love slipping into the sphere of the unconscious in order to insure its potency; the second, by supposing the predominance of an ever watchful self-love that instinctively reacts on the basis of egocentric motives, denies the very spontaneity that Sartre reaffirms. Together the two texts make it clear that the silent presence of of self-love in the fabric of perception poses a significant restriction upon the freedom of consciousness, thus conditioning the facticity that Sartre considers absolute.

Even if the portrayal of self-love as personified desire had only metaphorical—and not metaphysical—value, the developments of the metaphor that depict self-love's internal blindness to the primacy of its own motivational power would show conclusively that, for La Rochefoucauld, the work of consciousness does not start from nothing, that it is carried out on the surface of a deep-running stream, is channeled, as it were, by a mysterious and unfathomable undercurrent of unconscious activity. In the emergence of self-love we have noted the unidirectional movement of this submerged consciousness, which could not turn back upon itself and attain self-consciousness without deforming or canceling out the projection of desire of which it is a product and a function. For La Rochefoucauld it is precisely the movement of nonpositional consciousness, whether immediate or submerged, that is "contaminated" from the outset by drives of aggression and absorption. Only at the level of self-conscious understanding can the innate patterns of egotistic response be diverted and the possibility of altruistic conduct established. Thus Sartre's objection to La Rochefoucauld's psychology takes the categorical form of a diametrical opposition: pure, totally undetermined consciousness evolving toward self-contamination through self-awareness versus impure, partially determined consciousness evolving toward self-purification through self-awareness. This opposition parallels Sartre's opposition to Freud and denotes succinctly what is pre-Freudian in La Rochefoucauld.[34]

These conflicting images of consciousness mark a significant difference in the mode and power of psychological explanation.

34. To be sure, the distance separating La Rochefoucauld from Freud remains great. While Masson-Oursel insists especially upon the nonclinical motivation of the moralist's reflection, the distinction most pertinent to the present argument stems from La Rochefoucauld's single-minded concentration on the acquisitive instinct of self-love to which the unconscious is subservient. Freud's attention to the multiplicity of instincts and his effort to chart the unconscious in its full complexity, as a separate scene of action, decisively narrow the scope of meaningful analogies.

On the one hand, the Sartrean view disallows any direct intrusion upon the freedom of consciousness, thereby blocking off the sphere of behavioral explanation at the level of identifiable influences that condition the choices open to conscious election. Analysis bears upon the activity of consciousness, showing how it determines the choices that are made. On the other hand, the postulation of an unconscious provides a modality through which direct influence upon conscious activity is mediated. This allows for an order of a posteriori explanation—an explanation capable of encompassing the acts of consciousness—which cannot occur under the auspices of existential psychology. Analysis bears upon the whole personality, revealing the extent to which conscious activity is determined. While the exclusion of an unconscious from the conception of the personality may appear to add strength to the underpinnings of an ethic, its inclusion reinforces the extension of psychological understanding.

But can one believe that La Rochefoucauld promotes such understanding for any reason other than his concern with moral deprecation? Is there any motivation for divulging the autonomous perception displayed by self-love other than a desire to underscore the inherence of man's moral abjection? There can be no question of flatly denying such a motivation; it is rather a question of denying that there is *solely* a self-serving moralistic motivation, of affirming the polyvalence of concern in the moralist's enterprise. When La Rochefoucauld argues that the sources of illness lie in the passions and mental suffering, irreverently speculating on the infectiousness of love (Réfl. XII, "De l'Origine des Maladies"), the ethical disqualification of the patient is no more than an incidental (or underlying) message, mitigated if not compromised by the further implication that such illnesses are avoidable and that men can be reproached for allowing them. The manifest concern of the reflection is to connect some physical conditions to mental causes, inverting the recurrent practice of designating physical causes for mental effects. By no means does La Rochefoucauld's critique of human pretense require adding some more or less psychopathological insights in order to substantiate an already merciless skepticism in regard to man's ethical competence. On the contrary, recognizing in concrete terms the influence that the mind may exert over the body has essentially the same implication as recognizing the influence of the unconscious, for the view from any point in the dialectic of mental and physical energy leads back to the fundamental question that La Rochefoucauld's psychology raises: the extent to which the mind has control over *itself*, whether in dealing with influences on itself or in exerting influence outside itself.

Although this question most often arises in an essentially moral context (embracing the problem of responsibility, the judgment of actions, and so forth), it also appears, as in Réflexion XII, as a matter of intrinsic interest in a strictly observational context, devoid of didactic overtones. Moreover, even in those cases where the implication of man's ethical disqualification is overt, an accusation of moralistic bias is exceedingly difficult to formulate persuasively, if only because the observations do stand independently and do not fall automatically under the governance of another conceptual order. It is much closer to the spirit of the *Maximes* and the *Réflexions* to insist upon the attempt to ground a moral position in psychological understanding, to attach the development of a rudimentary psychology to the supposition that assessing man's potential for self-control is a precondition for resolving questions of moral judgment. Undeniably, the accent of psychological insights in these books is usually negative, pointing to limits and constraints. The potential for positive action is almost never recognized in psychological terms; it remains as imprecise as the relationship between desire and self-consciousness in self-love. Yet the crucial question is raised and brought into focus, and insofar as that question posits a fundamental concern with the problem of self-control, it governs the moralist's more positive reflections on society and ethics.

3 The Social Ethic of *Honnêteté*

It has been said that La Rochefoucauld adopts psychology as his prime field of investigation;[1] it is no less evident, however, that his psychology, and especially the theory of self-love, is inextricably intertwined with the elucidation of human relationships in society. As previously noted, the psychological insights of the *Maximes* and the *Réflexions* open onto a sociological perspective in at least two respects. First, the observation of human motivations appears to be on firmer ground in a social sphere, where the ego of the observer is less immediately involved than in introspective analysis. Second, it is in the social sphere that man's efforts to exert control over himself and his environment can be observed and evaluated. Once the individual is placed in an interpersonal situation, the comprehension of egocentric activity becomes, to be sure, more complicated. To perceive man as a creature of self-love is to detect, over and beyond his fidelity to possessive instincts, the critical influence that other people exert upon his conduct and to appreciate the difference between a man acting by himself and the same man acting

1. Dominique Secretan, ed., *Réflexions ou sentences et maximes morales* and *Réflexions diverses* (Geneva, 1967), introduction, p. xxiii: "Psychology, the science of human adjustment, is indeed La Rochefoucauld's field of inquiry."

under observation.[2] As a factor in the determination of a course
of action, the anticipated response of witnesses functions as a
coercive presence to which man's capacity for action can ordinarily be traced: "Perfect valor consists in doing without witnesses what one would be capable of doing before the world at
large" (Max. 216). Such perfect valor is rare (see Max. 213,
215); it requires a man capable of acting virtuously on his own,
for himself; it supposes a degree of independence and self-
control that La Rochefoucauld associates with the mythical
élévation of the hero (cf. Max. 217), whose ethical purity requires the exclusion of public opinion from his concerns.

Beneath the *Maximes* and the *Réflexions* some readers sense
an uneasy ambivalence with respect to the hero, who appears as
the object of both exaltation and demystification.[3] The prevailing current of La Rochefoucauld's thinking does, without
question, lead away from adherence to a heroic outlook and
toward a practical decision to come to grips with the particular
characteristics of human nature that determine societal normal-
ity. Over and over the *Maximes* invoke, as matters of fact,
the fundamentally egotistical motivations that govern human
relationships.

Self-love increases or decreases the good qualities we see in our
friends in accord with the degree to which we are satisfied with
them; and we determine their worth by the way they get on with us.
[Max. 88]

2. Cf. Charles Andler, "La Rochefoucauld," in *Les Précurseurs de
Nietzsche*, 3d ed. (Paris, 1920), p. 190.
3. See in particular Henri Coulet, "La Rochefoucauld et la peur d'être
dupe," in *Hommage au doyen Etienne Gros* (Gap, 1959), pp. 107–11. Other
notable studies on La Rochefoucauld and heroism: Paul Bénichou, *Morales
du grand siècle* (Paris, 1948), ch. IV, and Pierre-Henri Simon, *Le
Domaine héroïque, des lettres françaises* (Paris, 1963), pp. 181–92. La
Rochefoucauld's view of the hero merits attention primarily in the context of
his ethical stance. The psychological and sociological insights into the hero's
position vis-à-vis other egos (*stulti*) provide indisputable corroboration of
Bénichou's thesis, according to which La Rochefoucauld denies the viability
of the heroic posture in the context of a wider critical examination of the
declining aristocracy.

Humility is often just a feigned submissiveness, used to gain the submission of others; it is an artifice of pride which lowers itself in order to gain ascendancy; and although pride transforms itself in a thousand ways, it is never better disguised and more capable of deceit than when hiding behind the face of humility. [Max. 254]

These maxims represent two sides of the same coin, man's self-serving judgment of others and his self-protecting concern to manage the judgments to be conferred upon him by others. In each case, self-love instinctively assumes the right to subject (*soumettre*) others, to give priority to its own centrality and satisfaction in preference to fair judgment and genuine understanding. Maxime 254 marks emphatically the deceptive capability ("*feigned* submissiveness," "*artifice* of pride," "better *disguised* and more capable of *deceit*," "*hiding* behind the face") that self-love deploys when faced with its counterpart in other men.

Acquiring the pervasive force of an unquestioned habit, the social pattern of deception naturally carries over into the psychological pattern of self-deception. The latter is rooted in the internal histrionics of a deceitful self-love that escapes direct awareness and fosters man's false perception of his own motives: "We are so accustomed to disguising ourselves from others that we end up disguising ourselves from ourselves" (Max. 119). By the same token, one can suspect man of profiting from his mastery of self-deception as he goes about deceiving others: "What shows that men know their own faults better than one may think is that they are never mistaken when heard discussing their own behavior: the same self-love which ordinarily blinds them then opens their eyes and gives them such clear perceptions that they are led to omit or to disguise the slightest things which might be condemnable" (Max. 494). Here we catch the outlines of a simple dialectic between the public and the private self within which the degree of self-deception decreases as the concern with deceiving others increases, and vice versa. Even if openly exposed in a momentary lucidity required by social circumstance, self-love can expect to recuperate its guise of secrecy upon the return to privacy.

Thus the scheming of self-love situates man in a role—deceiver of self, of others, of self and others together—and sets in motion a social comedy revolving around the confrontation of conflicting egotistical drives.[4] The nature of social interaction has to be redefined in terms of the predominant and ubiquitous pursuit of private interest: "What men have called friendship is merely an association, a reciprocal balancing of interests, and an exchange of good offices; it is finally just a business arrangement in which self-love always envisages something to be gained" (Max. 83). On a purely semantic level, this maxim plays off a conventional concept (*amitié*) against other, more empirical notions in a verbal conflict, the result of which is the debunking so characteristic of the *Maximes*. Viewed in terms of game theory,[5] word games of this type throw into question the relationship between linguistic signs and the realities they

4. The enacting of this social comedy can, of course, be represented in various ways. Rousset, who insists upon the heart's propensity to deceive the mind, views self-love as destructive of any genuine human community and suggests that human relations thus appear to be essentially a psychological comedy in which man remains a solitary creature who merely plays the role of classicism's "social being." (See "La Rochefoucauld contre le classicisme," *Archiv für das Studium der Neueren Sprachen*, 180 [1942]), 107–112. A. J. Krailsheimer ties the "social aesthetic" to the impossibility of attaining the autonomy of the philosopher or the hero and says that the harsh necessity of social success in a society where political adventure had become impossible inevitably encouraged the "tendency towards play-acting" (*Studies in Self-Interest from* Descartes to La Bruyère [Oxford, 1962], pp. 82–83). Jean Starobinski relates the logic of a "new theory of the mask and the lie" to the discovery of the emptiness of being, a discovery that forces the man who seeks to *be* to construct his being with appearances ("La Rochefoucauld et les morales substitutives," *NRF*, nos. 163–164 [July/Aug. 1966], p. 39).

5. "La Rochefoucauld and the Rationality of Play," *Yale French Studies*, no. 41, "Game, Play, Literature," 1968. Hereafter, portions of this article will be integrated, with some adaptation, into the discussion of *honnêteté*. The first part of the article introduces the perspective of game theory, especially its concentration upon the structures of conflict, and applies it to linguistic games, envisaged as conflicts between words and concepts; the limited analogy subsequently developed between linguistic and social games depends upon the representation of the game as a conflict of interest. Cf. R. Duncan Luce and Howard Raiffa, *Games and Decisions* (New York, 1957).

purport to designate. The phrase "what men have called friendship" points to the temerity of naming any human conduct whatsoever, *dis*-plays the word in its fundamentally functional and relational, rather than representational, aspect and reminds us that for the interpreter of human behavior the referential function of language is continually problematical.

Yet as soon as we move beyond the perspective of verbal conflict to include the realities brought into question by the words, we realize that the referential function remains paramount in the moralist's statement—that, for example, friendship as a human relation is quite as problematical as the use of the term *friendship*. Certainly its existence as a real experience is not questioned. The suggestion is, rather, that our notion of friendship should be cleansed of fantasies and supported by hardnosed observation. This observation furnishes a version of interpersonal relationships that has intrinsic interest as a view of society. What is implied by the equivalence of four terms— *une société, un ménagement réciproque d'intérêts, un échange de bons offices, un commerce*—that form a sphere within which self-love is the driving force? To depict social intercourse as exchange, reciprocity, trading, arrangement, and so forth, amounts to underscoring its entrenchment in interchange and interdependence: communal existence inevitably constitutes an *economy*, within which the participants naturally pursue their own interests and in so doing tend to treat one another as adversaries, contestants seeking a reward: "Each person wants to find his own satisfaction and advantages at the expense of others; we always prefer ourselves over those with whom we seek to live, and we almost always make them sense our preference; this is what unsettles and destroys society" (Réfl. II, "De la société"). Social interaction appears to reproduce unceasingly an interplay of differing preferences within which individuals run the risk of upsetting society by following their egotistical impulses.

Rational understanding of this conflict of interest leads to what game theory terms a game of *strategy:* "Interest speaks all sorts of languages, and plays all sorts of roles, even that of the disinterested party" (Max. 39); "In all walks of life each person puts on an air and an outward appearance in order to look the way he wants others to believe that he is. Thus we can say that society is composed only of airs" (Max. 256). Unlike games of skill or games of pure chance, games of strategy require the player to assume a role that he conceives and acts out with regard to other players, who are likewise rational actors playing their roles. Thus the human comedy, staged in a world composed of guise and pretense where calculation presides over the acting, absorbs and accommodates a host of conflicting motivations (as many as there are players), each of which bypasses the dangerous (potentially tragic) clash of unmediated drives, anticipating the gain available with lower risk through ingenuity and artifice, relying upon the utility—and relative security— of controlled appearances.

Notwithstanding the pervasive empire of the traditional antitheses, appearance/reality, mask/truth, and the like, these categories acquire no substantive ontological status in the *Maximes.* Since maxim after maxim works to unsettle "realities" perceived at all levels of human experience, when the *Maximes* are viewed as a collection they seem to demonstrate almost endlessly that one debunking merely lays bare another notion to be reduced, that critical analysis can subvert any reality, even basic phenomena uncovered deep within the self. Although unmarked by didactic asseveration, a crucial lesson for society does arise from such destructive analysis: man must agree to deal with appearances, must accept the interplay of "truth" and artifice without arbitrarily depreciating the latter: "There are disguised falsehoods which represent the truth so well that not allowing oneself to be deceived would be an error of judgment" (Max. 282). The wise man chooses to play the game and does so willingly because he admits that the scandalous realness of appearances cannot be overcome. Rather than a hierarchical scheme based upon the axiological subordination of illusion to truth, we confront in society a game in which both participate as functions whose interplay will determine value, which—no longer preconceived as an immanent property of the "true"—relates to the quality of play and/or to the outcome of the game.

The emerging sociological reality here pertains not to the still vulnerable, metaphysically tinted essence or principle that exploded illusions leave exposed, but to the observable relationship between the factual and the fictive—it is the reality of their *jeu* (game, play, interplay, interaction, interacting), whose rules govern the ongoing concatenation of fact and fiction, disallowing the triumph of one over the other. Barren "essential" truth about men, were it accessible, would be unbearable, undermining all human contacts: "Men would not last long in social existence if they were not one another's dupes" (Max. 87). Conscious of his own reticence, the *honnête homme* tends to institutionalize a regulation of social relations, protecting the individual against inexpedient exposure: "The relation which can be found among minds would not uphold society for long if society were not *controlled* and *supported* by common sense, by good humor, and by the consideration which must obtain among persons who want to live together" (Réfl. II, "De la société," italics added). Regulating the perpetuation of mutual deception, the rules of *honnêteté* correspond to a strategy of cooperation or coalition designed to secure the pleasures of the game itself, to nurture the connection between minds by conditioning their (inter)play, forbidding subversive conquest: "The wise man finds greater advantage in forgoing battle than in winning" (MP 50). Yet solitude offers no escape from the search for an absolute truth: "It is sheer folly to wish to be wise all by oneself" (Max. 231). What then is the lot of the "wise dupe" who elects to play the game, to participate in society? Pursuing his interest through cooperation, each player enters into the jurisdiction of the game, commits himself to continue

playing, accords his undivided attention to the action, and resists at all costs the disillusion and isolation of either victory or
defeat. Caught up in their roles, the players incorporate—and
simultaneously incorporate themselves into—the dominion of
the game. Their renunciation of victory connotes a subtle triumph that ultimately belongs to the game itself, whose control
over all the forces in play sustains the enaction of a successful
social strategy.

Recognizing that La Rochefoucauld must be considered one
of the theoreticians of *honnêteté*, Bénichou traces his originality
to the experience behind the adoption of this relatively conventional position: "His originality is that he is aware, more than
anyone else, of the ruins upon which it is constructed."[6] This is
not to suggest, of course, that La Rochefoucauld's personal
sensitivity to the erosion of aristocratic values suffices in itself
to account for the particular articulation of the theory of
honnêteté that we find in the *Maximes* and the *Réflexions*. The
originality of this elaborative enterprise should also be related
to the possibility of drawing out the internal logic of these
works along two separate tracks. On the one hand, *honnêteté*
may represent a willful response, the last resort of lucid nobles
who seek to preserve their society from the iconoclastic menace
of a heroic thrust toward individual glory and self-fulfillment.
Numerous passages in the *Réflexions* lend credence to this idea.
On the other hand, the theory may be understood as directly
correlative to the theory of self-love insofar as it envisages the
practice of *honnêteté* as an instinctive tactic consistent with the
self's concentration upon its own preservation and dignity.
Taken together, these strains of analysis offer an intriguing
interplay of voluntaristic and fatalistic perspectives, a variation
of emphasis corresponding loosely to a fluctuation of viewpoint
between individual (psychological) and collective (sociological)
concerns. Regardless of the viewpoint, however, the advocacy

6. Paul Bénichou, "L'Intention des *Maximes*," *L'Ecrivain et ses trauvaux*
(Paris, 1967), p. 36.

of *honnêteté* reflects a logic of counteraction (not one of resolution or overcoming), for the *honnête homme* readily accepts a modus vivendi with aggressive and/or destructive tendencies and seeks to balance them through regulation rather than to eradicate or transform them. Within his highly polished, urbane community, he can engage simultaneously in verbal and social play, having the opportunity to bring both conceptual and interpersonal conflict under the control of endlessly renewable games.

Whether words or people, the "opponents" in these games are functionally interdependent, can only exist in *co*existence, as parts of a system wherein the adversary is also a partner and the "players" enter into an openly ambivalent relation corresponding to what Schelling terms a "mixed-motive game"[7]—an intersection of partnership and competition, concordance and contradiction. Beneath the conventions and tactics that allow the games to endure lie the structural axes of language and society, rules of grammar and rules of conduct, indispensable frames of reference for an analytic assessment of the quality of play. In their respective domains the rules both set limits and open possibilities: projecting a formal construct of boundaries, procedures, errors, and conventions, they provide the players with an opportunity to develop patterns of contention, to channel their conflicts into the realm of artistic expression, to deal with the threat of impotence or destruction by subjecting it to what Starobinski calls an esthetic transmutation, a displacement of moral imperatives by esthetic values.[8] La Rochefoucauld thus links the subduing of pessimism to a necesarily communal objective: to make social relationships, as well as verbal ones, a work of art, to judge an impoverished society and its players by artistic criteria instead of applying unattainable moral standards. Starobinski asserts that the recourse to artful play— to the diversion criticized by Pascal—is fully conscious, the choice of a disabused moralist: "The spirit of play, the concern

7. Thomas C. Schelling, *The Strategy of Conflict* (New York, 1963), p. 89.
8. "La Rochefoucauld et les morales substitutives," p. 211.

with elegance and exact expression will in no way change the
pessimistic conviction. They will only cover it over with a
veneer of hedonism."[9] Man remains fundamentally the aggressive creature of self-love, achieving his humanistic identity
only as a player in the ongoing game of cultural refinement.

It is self-evident that the principal instrument for playing this
game is language and that the play of the salon thrives on the
exhibition of elegance and subtle, precise expression. The fourth
of the *Réflexions diverses*, "De la conversation," reads like a
manual of strategy for permanent success in polite society,
treating skillful conversation as an end in itself, a gratifying
concurrence of social stability and genteel pleasures. As if to
crystallize the difference of La Rochefoucauld from Pascal,
Starobinski adopts the perspicuous formula "a wager for
speech,"[10] a commitment that not only precludes taking refuge
in divine mysteries but also discredits in advance any call to
practical action. Although language may enter into cooperative
efforts as an effective force, when discourse becomes a communal art cultivated by men as the crucial element of their
interrelations, language can assume a profoundly conservative
role in society. If we ordain that social intercourse be concen-
trated in verbal exchange, in a sort of fanciful or sportive nego-
tiation with the primary objective of preserving the advantages
of negotiating, we may derive a prolonged sense of satisfaction
from manipulating the multiple resources of language so as to
structure the functioning of society. Yet this institutionalized
exploitation of language summarily discounts much of society's
potential for compounding other relationships and activities. In
short, we may promote linguistic refinement at the expense of
meaningful social development.

Perhaps the crucial divergence tending to vitiate the correlation of linguistic games and social games lies in the relatively
greater mediative power of the rules of grammar vis-à-vis the

9. Ibid., p. 212.
10. Ibid., p. 214.

rules of conduct: the incomparable flexibility of language provides a unique instrument for absorbing, restructuring, and expressing conflict, whereas polite society presupposes telling circumstantial restrictions both on the nature and scope of conflict and on the identity of the players. This drift toward a narrowing of the social context (to the exclusive world of an articulate elite) suggests that the operational parallelism heretofore supposed between mixed-motive games in language and those in society breaks down precisely at the point where the games are perceived in their natural conjunction and interpenetration. Word games in society—social games in language: their integration obviously entails a reciprocal determination which language and society exert on one another. This interaction results in another, more complex mixed-motive game that redistributes the forces in play, polarizing conflict in society and mediation in language, evincing the predictable concentration of *free play* at the locus—in speech—where mediation occurs. Recognizing that the articulation of conflict in Maxime 83 goes beyond a mere challenge to the meaning(fulness) of a word, one might simply have supposed that the social game takes place in the extralinguistic reality that the maxim, as a vehicle of observation, evokes. The *Réflexions* make it clear, however, that the play with and on words does not merely take control of conflict within the maxim while referring to a comparable regulation of conflict in society, but that the word play actually implements the mediation of the social conflict, that it meets directly the dual requirement of developing checks and balances for social as well as conceptual oppositions. Responding concretely to the mediative power of language, the theory of *honnêteté* frequently takes the form of a theory of language use, plying the rules of the game not only to the conception of proper and appropriate speech, but also to the art of interpreting speech and refraining from speech:

One must say natural, easy, and more or less serious things according to the mood and inclination of the persons who are conversing, and

not press them to approve of what one says, nor even to reply. . . .
One must never put on airs of authority while speaking, nor use
words and terms more imposing than the things. One can hold to his
opinions if they are reasonable, but in doing so should never offend
the beliefs of others, nor appear to be shocked by what they have
said. . . . But if there is a great deal of art in speaking, there is no
less in keeping quiet. There is an eloquent silence, which sometimes
serves to approve and to condemn; there is a scornful silence; there
is a respectful silence. . . . [Réfl. IV, "De la conversation"]

One can speak (to friends) of things which concern them, but only
insofar as they allow it, and one must maintain great circumspection;
it is polite, and sometimes even humane, to refrain from penetrating
too far into the recesses of their hearts; they are often hurt by the
unveiling of all that they know, and are hurt still more when one
sees through what they do not understand. [Réfl. II, "De la société"]

Since they move beyond a straightforward penetration into
the deeper realities of other personalities and explicitly incorporate a knowledgeable assessment of that penetration, such
overtly normative principles of the theory of *honnêteté* shed a
curious light on the trenchant psychological insights of the
Maximes. They lead to the inescapable implication that the
sociology of La Rochefoucauld rests on a quasi renunciation of
his psychological perspicacity; or, more precisely, they suggest
that the sociological understanding supported by psychological
insight places significant restrictions on the use of the latter and
complies with these restrictions by integrating the articulation of
psychological insights into the linguistic play of the *honnête
homme*. In other words, the theory of *honnêteté* displaces the
uncompromisingly "pure" psychology of the theory of self-
love—articulated with obdurate severity in the *Maximes*—with
a "practical," circumstantially oriented psychology that stops
short of driving home every disarming lesson of acute discern-
ment. This restriction on the pursuit of demystification is all
the more certain to be observed because the "rules of the
game" in polite society do not merely discourage direct, indic-

tive intrusions upon another person's ego, but ultimately provide for a measured interpretation of and reaction to any
statement.

"The true gentleman ['honnête homme'] is never excited
['se pique'] by anything" (Max. 203). The import of this celebrated dictum allows for a dual appreciation of the role of
incisive maxims in the society of *honnêtes gens*. In addition to
circumventing, by virtue of its generality, some embarrassments
of pointedly personal reference, the maxim assumes, by virtue
of its distinctive form, the status of an artistic (or linguistic)
object, open to interpretive discussion. Once the maxim is
identified as a statement, it is possible to play with it without
taking it too seriously, without dwelling excessively upon its
stark implications. Perhaps the most important internal guide to
understanding La Rochefoucauld's work lies in the warning
against appearing to be shocked, which amounts to a warning
against being diverted from concentration on upholding the
quality of play—in the game of reading as well as in society.

While, in the last analysis, La Rochefoucauld accords a
certain logistical priority to sociological over psychological perspectives, this priority does not stem simply from the acknowledged necessity of society to human life. As the sole theater
in which life can be acted out for and with others and not just
experienced for oneself, society takes on an existence and a
character of its own that transcend the individual player, relegat-
ing him to support of the community and of social values: "The
man who thinks he can find within himself the wherewithal for
doing without everyone else makes a bad mistake; but the man
who thinks that others cannot do without him is still more
mistaken" (Max. 201); "As it is hard for several persons to
have the same interests, it is at least necessary, for the tran-
quility of society, that they not have opposing ones" (Réfl. II,
"De la société"). Inclusion in the community of *honnêtes gens*
requires a modicum of conformity from each member, whose
individuality will be protected primarily by his reserve, sec-

ondarily by the consideration that the others afford him. Admission to the game means playing a position or a part, as opposed to "being oneself," precisely because the private self does not automatically attune its interests to the pattern of acceptability that defines the area of public interest.

Despite the relatively modern note struck by the attribution of primacy to the social order, La Rochefoucauld's adherence to the theory of *honnêteté* upholds a profoundly reactionary view of society, consonant with the separatism of a cultural elite, a self-conscious community of disabused minds bent upon securing an equilibrium among egotists that will allow for an optimum of truth, freedom, and pleasure. The distinction of "les *vrais* honnêtes gens" epitomizes the alliance of cultural perfection with social exclusivism: "False *honnêtes gens* are those who disguise their failings to others and to themselves. True *honnêtes gens* are those who are well aware of their failings and admit to them" (Max. 202). As a special group, "les vrais honnêtes gens" presumably possess a moral superiority, attained by those whose mastery of the game engenders a confidence allowing them to air the truths of private identity— almost as if they were actors in a metatheatrical setting who regain some sense of the distance between themselves and their roles. The ambivalence of the term *honnête,* which clearly takes on a moral connotation in the second sentence of Maxime 202,[11] reflects a permanent tension within the theory of *honnêteté* between the choices of withholding or of expressing personal truths. The whole normative apparatus of the theory represents an attempt to divert the notion of honesty away from simple

11. In Jacques Truchet, ed., *Maximes* (Paris, 1967), see p. 51, notes 1–3. Since the key qualifier "vrai" can mean either veracious or authentic, the reading of this maxim turns out to be somewhat delicate, especially because the opening sentence might at first glance set the emphasis on truth versus falsehood. The crucial relationship, however, is the one between "vrai" and "connaissent," linking true *honnêteté* with lucidity and opposing it to indulgence in ignorance about oneself. The authentic *honnête homme* is the one who plays according to the rules with no illusions as to the realities that underlie the logic of the game.

candor toward civility in the social sphere, where the observance of diplomatic procedures should facilitate the free exchange of general opinions and objective truths.

Yet the exchange of private, confesssional truths and personal views unspotted by the falsehood of omission clearly requires a degree of confidence that can only prevail in a still smaller, more exclusive community of kindred spirits. In Réflexion V, "De la confiance," La Rochefoucauld emphasizes the necessity of singling out those persons in whom one can confide without restraint. Although trust is "the bond of society and of friendship," the opening characterization of trust via comparison to sincerity suggests that the frame of reference for "true" *honnêteté* is actually a model of intimate, rather than group, relationships. Common to the entire reflection is the assumption that the "true" *honnête homme,* in refusing to violate a confidence, whatever the price of his fidelity, must be a man of rare virtue and fortitude, must belong to a kind of moral elite. At any rate, the size of the elite seems destined to diminish when its members are themselves implicated in the exchange of truths.

Within this narrowing sphere of interpersonal contacts, the ultimate case is necessarily that of relationships between two individuals. And on the surface this seems to be a privileged case in La Rochefoucauld's meditation on human nature. Invoked in five of the nineteen *Réflexions diverses* and in some sixty-four maxims, the nature of love is, at least in its frequency, the most prominent theme of his work, which also devotes considerable attention to the nature of friendship.[12] Moreover, the

12. Cf. Edith Mora, *François de La Rochefoucauld* (Paris, 1965), pp. 54–55: "It has never been recognized that the principal theme of the *Réflexions ou sentences et maximes morales* is Love: among perhaps a hundred key words that we can identify, and even if we set aside everything dealing with the passions in general or with jealousy, the word *Love* is dominant in forty-three of them, the other key words hardly recurring in more than thirty." (My figure of sixty-four maxims is based on Pierre Kuentz, ed., *Maximes* [Paris, 1966], Introduction, p. 34, the table that includes under the heading *Amour* not just those maxims containing the word *amour* but also those which, in using the verb *aimer,* clearly deal with the subject.)

perceptions relayed by maxims dealing with love display such remarkable variety and acuity that La Rochefoucauld has been typed "the first clinician of love,"[13] a worthy predecessor of Stendhal and Proust.[14] Yet the real significance of intimate relationships in La Rochefoucauld's work has to do with the latent consent, within the theory of *honnêteté*, to a necessarily narrow conception of community. As in the case of social relationships, the value of close personal relationships derives from their role in man's efforts to balance or divert the forces of selfish instincts and to attain a measure of humanity. These efforts presumably have a better chance to achieve permanent, deeply satisfying success and to attain a high degree of honesty (in the sense of veracity) when channeled into the sphere of love and friendship.

If there is one indubitable lesson to be garnered from La Rochefoucauld's meditation on love and friendship, it is simply that even very private relationships cannot easily transcend the natural patterns of human behavior. In a reflection remarkable for its emphasis on the passage of time (IX, "De l'Amour et de la vie"), the correlation between the temporal experiences of love and those of life suggests that many of the moralist's pronouncements on the nature of love may be treated as analogues to comparable insights into life, or vice versa:[15]

Love is an image of our life: each of them is subject to the same about-faces and the same changes. . . . This involuntary inconstancy is an effect of time, which in spite of us makes itself felt in love as in our lives. . . . Jealousy, mistrust, the fear of growing weary, the fear of being abandoned are troubles which accompany the aging of love, as illnesses accompany the excessive duration of

13. Jean Rostand, "La Rochefoucauld," *Hommes de vérité*, 1st series (Paris, 1942), p. 211.
14. The *rapprochement* with Stendhal is established by Pierre Moreau in "Les Stendhaliens avant Stendhal, I—Le Stendhalisme des classiques," *Revue des cours et conférences* (30 jan. 1927), p. 308 (cf. Truchet's introduction, p. lvii).
15. Felix R. Freudmann, "La Rochefoucauld and the Concept of Time," *Romance Notes*, III, 2 (1962), 34.

life: one no longer feels alive because he feels sick, and one no longer has the feeling of being in love except by feeling all the pains of love. (Réfl. IX)

Beyond its status as a mode of correlation, the march of time is recognized as an active force in this reflection, for it *puts its hold* on love and life, which are *subjected* to the irreversible process of change. Thus, as Freudmann points out, the effects of time enter La Rochefoucauld's arsenal of critical tools alongside the effects of self-love and other natural forces.[16] In combination, the various implements for debunking supply the impetus for a disenchanting picture of love, marred by impurity, futility, and suffering, or still worse, a hypocritical exercise of intrigue and coquetry.

Nevertheless, La Rochefoucauld fails to maintain a uniformly skeptical view of love, allowing a certain ambivalence to creep into it by admitting the possibility of *"le véritable* amour": "As for true love it is like the apparition of the spirits: everyone talks about them, but few people have seen any" (Max. 76; see also Max. 376, 473, 477).[17] Although the definition of love proves to be difficult (Max. 68), there are occasional, if somewhat indirect, statements that associate it with the "passions violentes" (Max. 266, 466) or "belles passions" (self-portrait), as an irrational and miraculous attraction, endowed with the strength to be lasting: "The same resoluteness which helps ward off love also serves to make it violent and lasting, and weak persons, who are always stirred up by the passions, are almost never really possessed by them" (Max. 477). In addition to the force of passionate desire, steadfastness in love demands a capacity for renewal, for the *re*-generation of passion:

16. Ibid.
17. The following discussion provides only a brief sketch of La Rochefoucauld's views on love, which have been extensively treated elsewhere. See in particular May W. Butrick, "The Concept of Love in the Maxims of La Rochefoucauld," Ph.D. dissertation, State University of Iowa, 1959; Robert Kanters, in La Rochefoucauld, *Oeuvres complètes,* Bibliothèque de la Pléiade (Paris, 1964), pp. xi–xii; and Corrado Rosso, *Virtù e critica delle virtù nei moralisti francesi* (Turin, 1964), pp. 19–21.

"Constancy in love is a perpetual inconstancy, owing to which our heart is drawn to all the qualities, one after another, of the person whom we love, sometimes giving preference to one, sometimes to another; so that this constancy is just an inconstancy which has been arrested and confined to the same object" (Max. 175; see also Max. 75, 176). Not that love is solely an affair of the heart, for all the inventive power of self-love comes into play: "An *honnête homme* can love life like a madman, but not like a dolt" (Max. 353). By no means, however, does the intellectual or spiritual component of love—"in the mind it is mutual understanding" (Max. 68)—override the predominance of self-love, which triumphs in the fulfillment of desire and in the pleasure of its own passion, not in the passion that it provokes (Max. 259, 262).

If, then, love seems perfectly compatible with self-interest, what makes it so rare? In the first place, the birth of a burning mutual passion is a matter of chance; then, in the long run, the maintenance of love requires that it be genuine, not staged: "Where there is love, no disguise can hide it for long; neither can love be feigned where there is none" (Max. 70; see Max. 74). Recognizing that "love's greatest miracle is to cure coquetry" (Max. 349; cf. Max. 376), La Rochefoucauld links the miracle of love to a withdrawal from the artifice of play. The truth of love lies in the bond of confidence and sincerity, in that "openness of heart" which, instead of a "subtle dissimulation for drawing the confidence of others" (Max. 62; cf. Max. 116), is "a love for truth, a repugnance for disguise, a desire to overcome one's faults, and even to diminish them by virtue of admitting them" (Réfl. VI, "De la confiance"). Here again it is clear that egotistical motives are not totally suppressed, since sincerity allows one to fulfill a desire for absolution or moral elevation; what is suppressed is the dependency on rules, the sense of restraint and "justes limites" that the intersection of multiple interests imparts to less intimate relationships of trust. When, in love, the power of egotism reaches its apogee (Max. 262), self-love arrives at the stage that allows it to give up its histrionic stance in favor of free play and to identify directly with its passion. The ultimate, if transitory, miracle of the love relationship is to harbor the coexistence of unfettered passion and candor, to achieve interpersonal harmony without normative regulation and in conjunction with unmitigated self-satisfaction.

True love opens the way to a kind of liberation, an occasion to "be oneself." Can the same be said of true friendship, to which La Rochefoucauld apparently attaches still greater value?[18] Two facts make this a surprisingly delicate question. First, in its consistency and uncompromising tone, the debunking of friendship surpasses that of love, leaving us with the barest minimum of suggestions as to the nature of true friendship. Second, "la véritable amitié" is invariably invoked concurrently with "le véritable amour"—"However rare true love may be, it is still less rare than true friendship" (Max. 473; see Max. 376, Réfl. XVII). Furthermore, in Réflexion XVII ("De l'inconstance"), the comparison of friendship to love (an analysis of the latter providing the basis for the comparison) unequivocally rules out the notion that men should prefer friendship because it is more durable than love: "But time, which changes temperament and interests, destroys each of them in almost the same way. Men are too weak and too given to change to sustain for long the weight of friendship." Confronted with the extreme rarity of true friendship and a host of unsettling insights into the falsities and weaknesses of common friendship, one can only proceed, at least for the most part, to envisage true friendship negatively in terms of what it is not, especially since the absence of violent passion in friendship works to restrict the analogy of friendship and love.

18. "A true friend is the greatest of all goods and the one which we are least concerned with acquiring" (MP 45). It is customary to recall, with respect to true friendship, La Rochefoucauld's relationship with Mme de Lafayette (cf. Bernard Pingaud, *Mme de Lafayette par elle-même* [Paris, 1959], pp. 28–29, 39 ff.).

As Truchet points out, our main guidepost in this area is this single maxim, "which dates from 1678, [and] gives, in short, La Rochefoucauld's ultimate thought on friendship":[19] "We can love nothing except in relation to ourselves, and we are only following our taste and our pleasure when we prefer our friends to ourselves; it is nevertheless by this preference alone that friendship can be true and perfect" (Max. 81). In friendship as in love, egocentricity remains the fundamental factor; yet friendship differs from love in one crucial respect—it does entail a real preference for the friend, whereas in love the lover continues to prefer himself: "There is no passion in which love of oneself reigns so powerfully as in love; and we are always more inclined to sacrifice the tranquillity of our loved one than to lose our own" (Max. 262). If sincerity and perfection in friendship are difficult and rare, it is because they require a strong commitment from self-love to achieve satisfaction through its capacity for self-denial and devotion to others rather than to cultivate intense passion or to pursue the self-centered promotion of a praiseworthy self-image. For the moralist who enunciates this principle of friendship, there is clearly no way to cleanse friendship of all egotism, to achieve pure altruism. True friendship, in order to avoid the hypocrisy and inconstancy discovered in the *Maximes* behind "what men call friendship," must embody a directed egocentricity, lucidly affirmed and, in the company of an equally lucid friend, shamelessly relished. The force and sustenance of such friendship depend upon a rare combination: two individuals whose tastes and pleasures coincide. For it is precisely in the solidarity achieved by sharing one's egotism with another, by perceiving and experiencing it in and through the other, that self-satisfaction can attain its fullest authentication. Just as the *honnête homme* accepts, in society, the realness of appearances, he accepts, in friendship, the inescapable truth of egotism. Whereas in society he casts his lot for the ego-shielding interplay of truth with illusion, in friend-

19. Introduction, p. 25, note 2.

ship he cultivates a less prescriptive, less distracting game, the
ego-building interplay of selfishness and selflessness, which is
the reality of unmitigated personal truth. The triumph of sustaining this truth in friendship is reserved to individuals who
find in themselves, without support from societal sanctions,
sufficient strength to keep their egotism under control. Whence
the extreme rarity of this exceptional achievement, securing in
the narrowest of human relationships the bond through which
honnêteté and veracity ultimately coincide.

If La Rochefoucauld's work holds out precious little hope for
attaining "real" love or friendship, does it not put forth the
solution of *honnêteté* as a kind of compensation, a more reasonable goal? To the somewhat simplistic thesis according to which
the theory of *honnêteté* represents a positive outcome of La
Rochefoucauld's thinking and at least a partial antidote to his
so-called pessimism,[20] one can obviously oppose the arsenal for
debunking that the *Maximes* assemble. Countless texts restate
the judgment that man is too weak, ignorant, and inconstant to
play the game of social adjustment consistently, to persist in the
exercise of prudence or honor. Nevertheless, since the solution
of *honnêteté* is developed in sociological terms, it is against the
background of society that it must finally be tested. The artisans
of polite society ultimately ignore the pessimistic implications
of their recourse to a cultural and/or moral elite, to a com-
placently antisocial perspective that overlooks the plight of
humanity while legislating the satisfaction of a happy few. As
Le Rochefoucauld depicts it, the standard of the *honnête homme*
makes such great demands upon its bearers that it remains out
of reach to the average egotist,[21] holds out little real hope for
"humanization." While acknowledging the potential for controlling self-love through the checks and balances of social interaction, the theory of *honnêteté* does not give form to a

20. Bénichou, *L'Ecrivain*, p. 5, note 5, provides a succinct survey of critics
(Moore, Adam, Kanters, Hippeau, Rosso) who are more or less aligned
with such a thesis.
21. Cf. pp. 7–8 of Kanter's introduction to the Pléiade edition.

societal design capable of reversing the broader implications of
the theory of self-love, for the latter sets forth a psychology of
Man in general, whereas the theory of *honnêteté* presents, not
a sociology of Man, but a social creation—historically precarious—of privileged men.

For the individual, the unresolved tension between the general theory of self-love and the particular theory of *honnêteté*
gives rise to an ethical dilemma. To ply oneself to the regimen
of *honnêteté* (and even more, to act with heroism) is at once
to commit oneself to a laudable search for human perfection
and to succumb to an egological drift toward alienation. To opt
for elevation is, in a restricted sense, to opt against humanity,
to ground a claim of superiority to those who remain victims
of their egotism. Faced with this choice, which eventually exposes the moralist to the charge of bad faith, La Rochefoucauld
unequivocally elects to pay the price of distinction, and in so
doing, implicitly posits the conjoint expression and sublimation
of the ego as the primary moral act upon which an ethic can be
built. Abstracted from the immediate historical setting in which
it was elaborated, the code of *honnêteté* can still be read as en-
abling legislation, as a general call for adherence to a program
for cultural upliftment. At any rate, La Rochefoucauld's ethic
should not be dismissed as the mere corollary of social elitism,
but should be examined as a response to the difficulty of opening the possibilities of moral conduct in the face of the constraints imposed by self-love.

The *Maximes* contain only a small number of precepts concerned with deportment.[22] The *Réflexions,* however, in elaborating the theory of *honnêteté,* necessarily include many normative statements, most of which reflect an overall concern

22. Truchet counts eight: Max. 66, 106, 174, 343, 392, 418, 434, 453. The
refusal to construct a normative ethic may be viewed as a reflection of La
Rochefoucauld's opposition to traditional moralizing, e.g., of his distaste for
the precepts of the Stoics. A more radical interpretation might posit, behind
this refusal, the assumption that framing a consistent ethic to which men
can adhere is impossible.

with securing harmony in human relationships. The code of prudence and self-control developed in the theory of *honnêteté* sanctions the practice of consideration and indulgence for others: "We must stand ready to excuse our friends when their faults were born with them and when these add up to less than their good qualities; we must often avoid revealing to them that we have noticed their faults and been shocked by them, and we must try to act so as to enable them to correct them [see also Max. 319]. . . . We should seek our own contentment and that of others,[23] make allowance for their self-love and always refrain from offending it" (Réfl. II, "De la société"). The explicit point of departure for the enunciation of these precepts is man's inclination, which the achievement of true friendship has to reverse, always to prefer himself to his fellow men: "We should at least know how to hide this preferential desire, since it is too natural in us for us to get rid of it" (Réfl. II). Within a reflection based on the premise that society is necessary to man, this acknowledgment that covering up the self-preference is necessary to society draws the connection between the theories of self-love and *honnêteté*. In the context of the social comedy, it clearly implies the moral acceptability of the mask.

As we might well expect, however, La Rochefoucauld hardly allows the social necessity of play to take on the semblance of a moral absolute, for here again a measure of theoretical caution intervenes to establish limits and constraints that govern the recourse to dissimulation and the scope of its use: "Complaisance is necessary in society, but it must have limits: it becomes a servitude when it is excessive; it must at least appear to be free, and when we comply with the opinion of our friends, they must be persuaded that we are also following our own opinion" (Réfl. II). This proposition terminates a substantial

23. The variant of the Gilbert edition (coll. des Grands Écrivains de la France, Paris, 1868–1893; and see Truchet, pp. 177–82, for an explanation of the textual problems) suggests even greater self-effacement: "Il faudrait faire son plaisir *de* celui des autres . . ." (We should make our contentment *of* that of others . . . [italics added]).

paragraph that focuses on the importance of maintaining enough distance from society to conserve one's personal freedom, to uphold respect for the individual and his private identity. What should impress the player who sets out to conform to this part of the code of *honnêteté* is the way in which tacit recognition of independence as a human value is carried over into the realm of appearances: necessary amenity must appear free. This apparent contradiction mirrors the wider contradiction assumed by the *honnête homme* when he adopts the devices of playacting in order to facilitate the exchange of truth and frank opinion. By requiring this incongruity of appearance and reality, the code marks the inescapable precedence of basic ethical values, calling for disinterested judgment and action, with which the social and esthetic values of polite society should not openly conflict. Far from displacing such traditional virtues as honesty, sincerity, trust, generosity, independence, and so forth, the normative enterprise of the *Réflexions* represents an attempt to legislate conditions within which they can be put into "practice" and be said to govern human conduct. Just as the code of *honnêteté* works to further both honesty and civility, it favors the advance of humanity in both a moral and a cultural sense, disallowing the pursuit of the esthetic at the expense of the ethical, and vice versa.

In principle, then, it should be possible to attach a positive moral value to the practice of *honnêteté*, which has frequently been identified as La Rochefoucauld's definitive ethical doctrine.[24] A reading of the *Maximes*, though, does not allow such

24. In addition to the articles by Bénichou and Starobinski, see Julius Schmidt, "Die Maximen von La Rochefoucauld," *Zeitschrift für französische Sprache und Literatur*, LVII (1933), 221–29. I do not propose to take up the question of Epicurean influences in La Rochefoucauld's ethic of *honnêteté*, although some of the possible *rapprochements* are rather convincing. The question receives an excessively simplistic treatment in W. Sivasryananda, *L'Epicurisme de La Rochefoucauld* (Paris, 1933); a far more insightful approach to the problem will be found in Louis Hippeau, "La Vertu épicurienne selon les Maximes de La Rochefoucauld," *La Table Ronde*, 103–104 (July–Aug. 1956), pp. 198–207 (reprinted in Hippeau, *Essai sur la morale de La Rochefoucauld*, Paris, 1967).

a view to pass uncontested: "However even the world of *honnêtes gens* lacks perfect wisdom, it is neither difficult nor meritorious to comply with its rules."[25] Coulet proceeds to invoke the hero's moral superiority over the *honnête homme,* arguing that the values to which La Rochefoucauld accords his ultimate allegiance pertain to a hero's view of humanity, one that discredits the false virtues of common mortals: "It is in the eye of that hero that humanity is self-love, vanity, the puppet of chance, blind passions."[26]

Moreover, with or without the stance of the hero, shedding doubt upon the moral value of the theory of *honnêteté* hardly exacts a herculean effort from the composer of maxims.[27] Since the theory is directed toward a conciliation of conflicting egos and includes neither discreditation nor approbation of self-love, its development can be attributed to the workings of self-love and interest that the *Maximes* expose—whence the possibility of deeming the code immoral in its very foundations. Of greater weight, to be sure, is the charge that *honnêteté* gives rise to a masquerade of false virtues, allowing its followers to content themselves with the facile artifice of virtuous action and thereby

25. Coulet, "La Rochefoucauld et la peur d'être dupe," p. 108.
26. Ibid., p. 110; see also Hippeau, "La Vertu épicurienne." Hippeau's interpretation recognizes that, by itself, an ethic of prudence and *obligeance* could never stand up under the critical assault that the *Maximes* launch against traditional moralizing. Thus, La Rochefoucauld's position would represent an advanced, fully disabused Epicureanism, in which the wise man accepts the impossibility of constant, unerring prudence and, in his wisdom, allows himself a modicum of folly: "If the wise man allows himself some foolishness through wisdom, however, he will do so with complete lucidity, recognizing this foolishness for what it is. He will give in to it, not because he believes in its truth, but simply in order to free certain forces that are simmering within him and that he cannot contain without suffering. Foolishness will be a game" (Hippeau, p. 205). As an objective basis for this Epicurean morality, Hippeau points to the value of hope, to which La Rochefoucauld would have attributed the value of a survival instinct, aligned with the fear of death (see Max. 504, MP 23). The resulting virtue, or *fausseté déguisée,* would employ the force of hope (see Max. 168) and the admixture of vice and virtue (see Max. 182), along with the outlet provided by "wise folly," in the sustenance of prudence.
27. See, for example, the majority of maxims dealing with moderation and prudence (Max. 17, 18, 65, 293, 308, MS 15, 34).

doing violence to the cause of "real"—and necessarily more difficult—moral uprightness. Insofar as resorting to false virtue creates still another triumph of self-love, these doubts about the moral value of *honnêteté* resolve into a single central question: does the critical appraisal of virtue in the *Maximes* hinge upon the advocacy of a *true* virtue that is incompatible with the prudential ethic of the *honnête homme?* In other words, does a higher, if not heroic, morality emanate from the *Maximes?*

The analysis of virtue stands out as the archetype of critical reduction in the *Maximes*. To define virtue is to expose the morally deficient nature of its source:

Our virtues are usually just vices in disguise. [Epigraph]

What we take for virtues are often just a collection of diverse actions and interests which fortune or our ingenuity is able to contrive; and it is not always through valor and through chastity that men are valiant and women chaste. [Max. 1]

What an Italian poet has said of the honor of women can be said of all our virtues: it is often nothing more than an art of appearing to be honorable. [MS 33]

What society calls virtue is usually just a phantom conjured up by our passions to which we give a respectable name in order to be able to do what we wish with impunity. [MS 34]

Now in each of these four texts we note that the restrictive *n'est . . . que* ("is . . . just," etc.) is itself restricted by an adverbial qualifier ("often," "usually"), which leaves open the possibility of an irreducible virtue. In some instances the use of the vice/virtue antithesis appears to imply the same possibility, suggesting that vice takes on the guise of virtue in imitation of something that is superior to and innately different from itself: "Hypocrisy is a tribute which vice pays to virtue" (Max. 218). By comparison however, vice clearly holds a more fundamental ontological position than virtue, if only because—

as the basic fact of "moral life"—it is never thrown into question. Virtue may consist of vice in disguise, but not vice versa, and only vice is represented as an inevitable experience of life:

It might be said that the vices await us in the course of life like hosts with whom we must stay one after the other; and I doubt that experience would lead us to avoid them if it were possible for us to pass two times along the same path. [Max. 191]

Nothing is so contagious as example, and we never do very good or very bad deeds which fail to inspire similar ones. We imitate good actions by emulation, and bad ones because of the malevolence of our nature, which shame held in check and which example sets free. [Max. 230; see also Réfl. VII, "Des exemples"]

At first glance, the image of vices as hosts (in Max. 191) may overshadow the larger image of the course of life, a conventional metaphor that incorporates the attentiveness to succession and to necessity that recurs throughout La Rochefoucauld's meditation on human experience. As a host, a vice is already present, waiting for errant men who have to accept its hospitality; and if a man, having already paid one visit to an evil host, nonetheless returns, his return does not merely reflect an innocent haplessness, for the necessity of the visit cannot depend simply on the availability of the lodging, but has to be seconded by the visitor's inborn inclination to evil—"the malevolence of our nature."[28] The distinction between imitating good actions by emulation and imitating bad actions by dint of human nature rests upon the referential disparity of the two adverbial phrases: "par émulation" picks up the notion of mimetic or competitive response, which the verb "imiter" carries over from the opening remark on the function of examples, whereas in the second half of the comparison "par la malignité de notre nature" is conceptually affiliated with the object

---

28. On the question of Jansenist influences in La Rochefoucauld's representation of good and evil, see Louis Hippeau, "La Rochefoucauld et les Jansénistes," *La Table Ronde,* 162 (June 1961), pp. 65–78 (reprinted in *Essai sur la morale de La Rochefoucauld*).

"mauvaises actions."[29] To turn this construction into a straight parallelism, it suffices to substitute for "par émulation" the notion that we imitate good actions "because of the *goodness* of our nature," but it is precisely this goodness that La Rochefoucauld is not prepared to concede without reservations: "It is quite difficult to distinguish goodness in all things, extended to everyone, from consummate cleverness" (MS 44). There is little need to illustrate La Rochefoucauld's (in)famous propensity to point out the contamination of goodness and virtue by interest, vanity, passion, or vice in general, a contamination that virtue naturally incurs because it can appear only in a corruptive atmosphere—in the course of man's recurrent dealings with the well-ensconced innkeepers of vice. The image of the hosts suggests that the predominance of vice over virtue or evil over good might well be represented in institutional terms; the former enjoys the unquestioned prerogatives of the establishment, while the latter has to confront the pull of absorption into the establishment.[30]

Although the cards are heavily stacked against the existence of real virtue, men continue to believe in it, or at least in their own: "What often prevents us from appreciating maxims which prove the falseness of the virtues is that we believe too readily that they are genuine in ourselves" (MP 7). Thus La Rochfoucauld's analysis takes him beyond the falsehood of virtues per se and points to the presence of falsehood—especially self-deception—in the process of assessing and reacting to virtue. The same individual who readily overlooks the flaws in his own supposed virtue will probably affirm those of his

29. A stylistic analysis would also note that the ellipsis of subject and verb prior to the object "mauvaises" is appropriate because the second adverbial complement no longer echoes the actions of imitation. The ellipsis effectively reinforces the association of the adverb with the object and thus prefigures the semantic predominance of the closing subordinate clauses.

30. Roland Barthes, ed., *Maximes et Réflexions* (Paris, 1961), introduction, pp. lxvii ff., describes the vice-virtue relationship as one between reality and appearance, within which the virtues are essentially parasitic and structureless. The vices, on the other hand, have at least the structure of energy, of the active principles that are indubitably real.

fellow men with unwarranted haste: "Quickness to assume
wrongdoing, without sufficient examination, is an effect of
pride and laziness: we want to find culprits, and we do not
want to go to the trouble of examining the crimes" (Max.
267). That the most fundamental moral or polemical structure
inherent to the analysis of virtue resides in the indictment of
inadequate understanding can be seen in the original version
of the epigraph (Max. 181 of the first edition): "We are preoccupied with our own advantage in such a way that we often
take for virtues what are actually just a number of vices which
resemble them, and which pride and self-love have disguised
from us" (see also MS 19). What is left out when this maxim
is geared down to the more categorical pronouncement of the
epigraph is not merely the clause referring to the source of the
disguise. The original text also places a more concerted emphasis on the misapprehension of virtue, that is, in addition to
disclosing the alliance of self-love with vice, the text points to
an excess of egotism, which is its inattention to itself. Man's
initial derelection consists in failing to see or in ignoring the
vitiating ingredient of self-love in the makeup of virtue. Men
cannot be guilty of their natural egotism, only of failing to
discern and restrain it. In exposing the fraudulent attitude that
men adopt toward virtue, the *Maximes* impugn their unwillingness to acknowledge the predominance of evil: "However
wicked men might be, they would not dare appear to be enemies of virtue, and when they wish to do harm to it, they
pretend to believe that it is spurious, or they attribute crimes
to it" (Max. 489). If they were honest, men would admit their
wickedness and carry out their opposition to virtue without
feigned disbelief or misrepresentation. Their distaste for the
beneficent acts of others (see Max. 14, 29) testifies to the
untimeliness of goodness and virtue in an interest-dominated
society.

As they expose man's hostile attitude to real virtue along
with his investment in false virtue, the *Maximes* seem to put

into practice the "ethic of lucidity" with which La Rochefoucauld is often associated. It is necessary to recognize, however,
that the virtue of lucidity could not constitute, by itself, the
real virtue that, in theory if not in fact, has to serve as the
counterpart to false virtue and as the positive pole in the vice/
virtue antithesis. Lucidity is but a starting point—an awareness
of egotism in which an ethic like the code of *honnêteté* can
well be grounded and back to which the *honnête homme* must
continually refer in order to maintain the moral integrity of his
position. True virtue, free from the inroads of vice, demands
the ability to appropriate the lessons of lucidity in opposition
to the prevailing force of vice. As we have come to expect, the
motif of authenticity is accompanied here, as in maxims that
invoke true love and friendship, by an awareness of its extreme
rarity and of the necessary possession of strength: "Nothing is
rarer than genuine goodness; the very ones who believe that
they possess it ordinarily have only weakness" (Max. 481).

Reflecting his skepticism toward the so-called "pacific virtues" (Max. 398; see also Max. 16, 169, 266, 293), the dissociation of true goodness from weakness invokes an important
leitmotiv of La Rochefoucauld's thought: "Weakness is more
opposed to virtue than is vice" (Max. 445; see also Max. 130,
316, 479).[31] Given the undeniable power of vice in the human
arena, virtue cannot stand up against it without commensurable

31. In connection with the debunking of passive virtues, the lone maxim
to raise directly the question of La Rochefoucauld's relationship to Christian
doctrine is especially noteworthy: "Humility is the authentic proof of
Christian virtue: without it we conserve all our faults, and they are only
covered over by the pride which hides them from others, and often from
ourselves" (Max. 358). In view of Maxime 254, which states that humility
is ordinarily feigned, the overall thrust of the *Maximes* can still be said
to run in the direction of debunking the Christian virtues in toto. In
addition, the insistence on force and will seems to suggest a kind of
supplementary debunking, for even if the Christian virtues, through the
presence of humility, proved to be genuine, they would not necessarily merit
the positive approbation reserved to the active virtues. One should doubtless
recall in passing that La Rochefoucauld's writing is deliberately profane,
humanistic in the full sense of the term. Whatever his private convictions
may have been (the debate refuses to close), his work manifests a decidedly
antitheological tendency.

strength: "No one deserves to be praised for goodness if he
lacks the force to be wicked: all other goodness is most often
just a laziness or an impotence of the will" (Max. 237; see
also MS 45). The vigor of denunciation in the *Maximes*
reaches its apex with the characterization of sloth, in an extraordinary text that deserves, stylistically and conceptually, to be
classed with the famous reflection on self-love (MS 1):

Of all the passions the one which is the least well known to ourselves
is sloth; it is the most zealous and the most malicious of all, although
its violence is imperceptible and its ravages are well hidden; if we
consider its power attentively, we shall see that in every eventuality
it assumes mastery over our feelings, our interests, and our pleasures;
it is the remora strong enough to stop the greatest ships, it is a calm
more dangerous to important affairs than reefs and the greatest
storms; the repose of sloth is a secret charm of the soul which
suddenly suspends the most ardent pursuits and the most unyielding
resolutions; to give in conclusion the true idea of this passion, it is
necessary to say that sloth is, as it were, a blissful state of the soul
which consoles it for every loss and which takes the place of its
every good. [MS 54]

The paradox of sloth, like that of self-love, stems from the
stealth of its activity, from its seeming ability to work mightily
and purposefully, that is, in contradiction to the observable
patterns of indolence. Not only does sloth achieve mastery over
opinions, interests, and pleasures, it can also prevail over the
violent passions, like love and ambition: "Sloth, however lan-
guorous, often exerts mastery over them nonetheless; it en-
croaches upon every aim and every action in life; it destroys
and consumes imperceptibly the passions and the virtues"
(Max. 266). Generating an inertia that dissipates the impulse
to purposeful exertion, sloth acts as the most insidious opponent
to virtue by consolidating in man the conditions under which
vice can predominate without challenge.[32] In a sense, as Barthes
points out, weakness and sloth represent a scandalous condition

32. Barthes introduction, p. lxxi. See Max. 1, 29, 121, 182, 185, 189, 218,
238, etc.

for La Rochefoucauld because they effectively put a stop to the dialectic of vice/virtue or good/evil and thereby exclude the very possibility of virtue. In the series of images that compose the second half of MS 54, each of the terms signifying an abeyance of movement ("rémore," "bonace," "repos," "béatitude") is modified by a complement that underscores the extraordinary braking power behind the realization of quiescence. The resulting picture of a listing, tranquilized soul offers a negative image of true virtue, which demands a soul with the strength to overcome the enticing comfort of inaction.

If there are, in reality, bona fide manifestations of such a forceful soul, one obvious reference point must be the glorious ascendancy of the hero: "Intrepidity is an extraordinary strength of the soul which raises it above the troubles, disorders, and emotions that the sight of great perils could stir up in it; and it is by dint of this strength that heroes maintain their inner calm and preserve the free usage of their reason in the most surprising and the most terrible eventualities" (Max. 217). Here the spiritual *force* of the hero serves to guarantee his freedom to commit moral acts, yet this is not to say that his intrepidity, any more than his lucidity, is thus qualified in ethical terms as *good*. On the contrary, the *Maximes* clearly recognize that inherently *great* action remains subject to post facto moral evaluation: "There are heroes in evil as in good" (Max. 185). The hero does not automatically serve as either the model or the judge of true virtue. As is the case with the code of *honnêteté*, the relatively evanescent evocation of heroism in the *Maximes* entails no full-scale redefinition of good and evil. For Nietzsche, who strongly approved of La Rochefoucauld's distaste for weak virtues such as pity, the moralist's critique of virtue failed to go far enough because it merely denied the truth of the motives behind actions, whereas Nietzsche went on to deny that moral judgments are founded upon truths.[33] Far from affirming the strength of the ego as a

33. *The Dawn of Day*, Frag. 103; *The Genealogy of Morals*, Frag. 362. Cf. Starobinski, "La Rochfoucauld et les morales substitutives," pp. 25–26.

fundamental value, the heroism invoked in the *Maximes* (and in the *Mémoires*) seems incommensurable with the energy cult of the Nietzschean overman. No more than the *honnête homme* can the classical hero, in striving for his own particular virtue, appropriate to his exceptional role, escape from the predominance of inherited values; at best, he can only hope to reorder them by assigning higher priority to heroic—*traditionally* heroic—values.

La Rochefoucauld, moreover, does not protect the presumed superiority of the hero from the barbs of critical deflation. He indicates that the hero's *élévation* can hardly stem from unique moral attributes since the ascent from the common to the heroic represents an essentially quantitative jump in ambition and vanity: "When great men let themselves be beaten down by long-drawn-out misfortunes, they reveal that they had only borne them through the strength of their ambition, not through that of their soul, and that apart from great vanity heroes are made like other men" (Max. 24). Rather than being an ethical assessment, this maxim brings into play what Starobinski terms "a principle of nonconservation of force,"[34] which is to say that heroism is undermined by temporal and material limitations on the generation of passions. The vanity of the hero does not, to be sure, constitute a moral disqualification; it reflects his lucidity with regard to his natural, inborn strength and goes hand in hand with his will to make use of that strength while he possesses it, a volition that separates him from the common lot of men who have "more force than will" (Max. 30).

The passive voice—"Les héros *sont faits*"—is a revelatory construction. Excluding the image of a self-made hero, it situates individual identity as a *product,* reflecting the predominance of natural endowment even in the heroic dimension. On the whole, commentators of the *Maximes* have failed to accord adequate attention to the difference between natural value and acquired value in La Rochefoucauld's outlook. Not only do the

34. "La Rochefoucauld et les morales substitutives," p. 33.

Maximes expose the being behind appearances, the man behind
the facade, they often proceed to qualify that being, to assess
the man in terms of his merit and his defects, his good and bad
qualities. This process reveals the crucial impact of nature's
selectivity in determining the individual's potential: "There
are good qualities which degenerate into faults when they are
natural, and others which are never perfect when they are acquired. We must, for example, use our reason to keep our
wealth and our counsel; but nature, on the other hand, must
give us goodness and valor" (Max. 365; see also Max. 53,
153, Réfl. III, "De l'air et des manières," and Réfl. XIV, "Des
modèles de la nature et de la fortune"). Thus it is necessary to
avoid confusing the qualifications of man's nature with the
judgment of his action. In large measure, the hero owes his
heroism to nature (and to fortune), just as man in general
owes to nature his limited potential for vice and virtue: "It
seems that nature has prescribed for each man, from the moment
of birth, limits for virtues and vices" (Max. 189; see also MS
36). Strictly speaking, it is within the range of this potential
for vice and virtue that moral judgment focused on the exercise
of reason comes into play.

On what basis, then, do the *Maximes* grant approval to
human action? The essential criterion calls for the exercise of
will, for "application" (Max. 243). Implicit in the definition
of *grandeur d'âme* (the antithesis of weakness or laziness of
the soul) as a function of *grands desseins,* and not as a fixed
preponderance of virtue over passion (MS 31), is the stipula-
tion that a praiseworthy act must carry out the conscious designs
of a naturally meritorious individual: "However astonishing
an action may be, it must not be considered great when it is not
the effect of a great aim" (Max. 160). This maxim states the
principle applied in others (Max. 7, 57, 120, for example)
where the discreditation of an action depends upon the individual's lack of conscious intent. Consonant with his insistence
on planning or calculation, La Rochefoucauld also shows con-

cern for the modes of action that are selected: "The glory of great men must always be measured against the means which they have used to acquire it" (Max. 157); "It is not enough to have great qualities; they must be well managed" (Max. 159; see also Max. 437). Maxime 157 clearly opens the way to a moral critique of heroism, making the hero subject to condemnation when he succumbs to the temptation to indulge wantonly in the exaltation of superior force. Rather than merely disallowing the possibility of justifying the means by the end, La Rochefoucauld affirms that the end must be measured against the means, that the individual should combine his talents with a view to controlling the relationship between the end and the means. Significantly, the final maxim in this group of texts (156–161) dealing with the value of conduct invites us to envisage this relationship in terms of proportionality: "There must be a certain proportion between actions and intentions if one is to derive from them all the results they can yield" (Max. 161). Hinged upon the search for effects, this text has an almost utilitarian ring: one may obtain a maximum of results from actions that correlate well with intentions—as if the desirability of proportion should derive, not from its intrinsic value, but from a concern with efficiency. What is ultimately sanctioned is nothing else than the deliberate regulation of forceful action.[35]

At first glance, the outlooks of the hero and the *honnête homme* seem to correspond in the commitment to lucidity that they both exhibit. Starting with this common denominator, it suffices to assent to the critique of heroism in order to arrive at

---

35. Rosso, *Virtù*, p. 26, affirms that the congruence of action and intention is the fundamental condition for positive judgment, but concludes, on the basis of Maximes 58 and 160, that such congruence is not to be found. This introduces a curious exclusivity into these texts, which seem to me to suggest primarily that man's judgment is often ill-conceived because he is unable to determine whether such congruence is present when he passes judgment on other men. At any rate, other texts make it clear that the criterion stated by Maxime 161 applies only within that area of activity where man is free to acquire qualities.

the conventional logic by which the hero's (La Rochefoucauld's?) application of lucidity to his own position in a changing society leads him to abandon the hero's role and to adopt
the more viable role of the *honnête homme*. To contest this
logic, however, it suffices to acknowledge, with Coulet, that
the *Maximes* question the viability of the *honnête homme* no
less than that of the hero. The alternative—heroism/*honnêteté*—
raised in a basically historical context, tends to obscure the
possibility of a less categorical view. If the exercise of lucidity
is situated in the sphere of moral judgment, the *Maximes* appear to gravitate toward a certain convergence of the decisive
modes of action—force and regulation—that distinguish, respectively, the lives of the hero and the *honnête homme*.

To this tentative synthesis it is doubtless pertinent to object
that the axiological statements cited earlier (among others,
Max. 157, 159, 160) refer uniformly, not to moral acceptability, but to greatness, and thereby imply an ineradicable preference for the supremely demanding, yet triumphant, virtue of
the hero. One has to recall—in answer to Coulet's dismissal of
honnêteté as well—that the *honnête homme* applies himself to
an exceedingly difficult regime, to the creation of a "*great
work*" (Réfl. II, "De la société"), thoroughly imbued with the
conscious design that La Rochefoucauld requires in great action.
Furthermore, the correlation of intent, action, and outcome
reaches an ideal culmination in the society of *honnêtes gens,*
where the goal of harmony—proportion between *actions* and
desseins—is attained by a veritable fusion of means and end in
the quest for linguistic perfection. By preserving his independence and intellectual detachment, the *honnête homme* retains
that crucial element of the hero's posture which guarantees the
free exercise of reason in trying circumstances—*il ne se pique
de rien.* By conceiving of *honnêteté* as an alternative to—and
not a replacement of—heroism, one can even think of the true
honnête homme as a superior individual who, relying less upon
the strength of his soul than upon the strength of reason, ex-

ercises in his own fashion the functions of a cultural hero. In his fashion he acquires a distinction that sets him above the lot of common men.

When, beyond its social significance, the meaning of *honnêteté* embraces moral connotations, the doctrine assumes its higher and more exclusive function as a summons to a certain authenticity. At this point, where the judgment to be rendered concerns the individual's manner of acquiring extrinsic traits and determining his place in life, both the hero and the *honnête homme* have to be measured by the same universally applicable standard, which cannot be narrowly qualified as either heroic or *honnête:* "I do not intend, by what I say, to enclose us so tightly within ourselves that we do not have the freedom to follow examples and to acquire useful or necessary qualities that nature has not given us: the arts and sciences are good for everyone; but these acquired qualities must have a certain relationship and a certain union with our own qualities, which extend and increase them imperceptibly" (Réfl. III, "De l'air et des manières"). Like the social ethic of harmony and gentility that it subsumes, this precept is essentially classical. Coinciding with the traditional theme of fidelity to one's nature, the authenticity in question here remains distant from the modern emphasis on accepting one's freedom and responsibility in opposition to the notion of a natural self.[36] Yet this hardly furnishes a legitimate basis for accusing La Rochefoucauld of using nature as a refuge from moral accountability. In the wake of his critical assault upon the inadequacies of man's natural qualities, he affirms both the freedom to acquire qualities that nature fails to provide and the necessity of doing so. The observation

36. Nearly all of La Rochefoucauld's recent commentators stress the motif of authenticity at some point, be it the authenticity of his quest for truth or the requirement of authenticity in the individual's conception of himself. Perhaps it is worthwhile to note explicitly that, to a large extent, this sense of authenticity stems from the tone and conceptual rigor of La Rochefoucauld's writing, and only secondarily from statements that directly concern the principles of judgment. In the last analysis, it is the writer's exercise of judgment that counts.

of men in action reveals the importance of controlling wisely this acquisition process: "It seems that men do not find enough faults for themselves; they still increase them in number with certain peculiar qualities with which they seek to adorn themselves, and they cultivate them with such care that they eventually become natural faults which are no longer within their power to correct" (Max. 493). This maxim, which links the display of discordant qualities (appearances) to a decisively reprehensible result, also suggests the possibility of developing natural merit, grounded in adherence to qualities that can be assumed without undue pretense. The call for a harmonious relationship between the natural and the acquired, which implicitly accords a sanction to the axiological precedence of *le naturel*, does not simply reflect the esthetic prejudice of polite society; it is, for the man who understands that developing such a relationship depends upon a candid perception and evaluation of his nature, a genuine call to honesty and integrity. The *Maximes* go no further than this, offer no delineable ethical system either in opposition or in parallel to that of the *Réflexions:* instead, they bring to bear upon the code of *honnêteté,* as upon heroism, a rigorous axiological perspective that underscores the consummate difficulty of achieving—over and beyond social distinction—moral rectitude.

4 The Formulation of Abstract Truths

The Insecurity of Knowledge

The preceding chapter works out a more or less coherent, more or less standard interpretation of the *Maximes* and the *Réflexions,* one that parallels in many respects other attempts to piece together for La Rochefoucauld a "consistent position," or to mark the limits of his consistency. In at least one important respect, however, this interpretation reflects a reading of these texts that departs from the approach of most other commentators: the moralist's position is not represented as a function of an intellectual itinerary, the steps of which can be traced in or deduced from the work.[1] Thus, for example, grasping the coherence of the *Maximes* does not depend upon identifying a variety of opinions that La Rochefoucauld might have held at various stages of his reflective experience and fabricating a *chronological* or sequential account of those opinions. Similarly, to relate the *Maximes* and the *Réflexions* is not necessarily to posit the logical priority of one over the other, or even to dis-

1. For an example of a particularly insistent construction of such an itinerary, see R. Grandsaignes d'Hauterive, *Le Pessimisme de La Rochefoucauld* (Paris, 1914).

sociate them at all in terms of their fundamental outlook on human nature.

By virtue of its discontinuous form and its cognitive force, the work of La Rochefoucauld puts up strong resistance to a reductive reading, to a reordering of its components; it challenges us to read it as an ensemble of statements, all of which are valid simultaneously. What these statements, in their plurality, leave to be worked out is not a single synthetic or conclusive statement, but the context of their validity. Thus the understanding of La Rochefoucauld's coherence depends neither upon the iconoclastic impulse of his critical insights nor upon the disabused wisdom to be gleaned from his formulation of normative principles. It originates in what might be considered an intermediate perception of his thought, stressing his attentiveness to the constraints attendant to the human condition, in particular, to the limits within which self-controlled action is possible. In the light of those limits, exhibiting the outlines of a denominable position seems relatively unimportant, needlessly academic. What matters is the attempt to formulate and to apply legitimate principles of judgment, to achieve in the conception of *honnêteté* and in the overall concern for proportionality a significant convergence of ethical and esthetic values. It is, then, in the effort to ply the notion of man to his naturally limited potential for willful action and to depict him as a creation subject to meaningful evaluation that the present reading has situated the unifying force of the moralist's enterprise.[2]

To contest the supposition that one can account for this critical enterprise in terms of a logical, evolutionary representation of La Rochefoucauld's thought is not to argue that it is illegitimate or useless to attribute an intellectual itinerary to

2. There is a remarkable concordance between this representation of La Rochefoucauld's outlook and the perspective set forth in the reflection "Du Faux." In La Rochefoucauld's corpus this text, too long to be quoted here, can be regarded as exemplary in the elaboration of *conditionality* as a kind of leitmotiv, i.e., the reflection displays both a thought that is characterized by the statement of conditions and requirements and a thought process that characteristically resorts to the conditional mode.

the author of the *Maximes*. Although studying the evolution of his works tends to bring out initially a process of artistic development, it should, in turn, illuminate the thought processes with which the practice of a style is correlated. The importance of such research is not, therefore, in question. If, however, it is correct to attribute to La Rochefoucauld an axiological perspective that subsumes his meditations on heroism and *honnêteté*, and if one is justified in setting his insistence upon man's subservience to uncontrollable forces within the context of an attempt to determine the limits of human potential and to delineate the sphere of assessable action, then there is cause for considerable skepticism toward interpretations that seek to explain the presence of supposedly incompatible positions in his work. Thus, for example, while the logical sequence suggested by Starobinski—critique of conventional morality, substitution of a heroic ethic, critique of the substitute ethic, substitution of a social esthetic—may correspond to an argument for which the *Maximes* and the *Réflexions* provide evidence and analytical support, it does not correspond to an argument that is marked within the text, nor does such an argument, with its neat progression that belies the dearth of logical ordering in the book, prove necessary to make it intelligible.

The dynamics of criticism and response invoked by Starobinski points, however, to an ultimate paradox of destructive criticism itself, which the absence of argumentative sequence makes more acute. Nothing in the *Maximes* indicates why or where the pursuit of critical negation should stop; nothing suggests that the process of demystification can ever get to the absolute bottom of things, can ground a claim to fully adequate knowledge: "In order to know things well, it is necessary to know them in detail, and since the detail is almost infinite, our knowledge is always superficial and imperfect" (Max. 106). Within a work that relentlessly calls attention to what men do not or cannot know (see Max. 80, 269, 295, 436, 439, 460, 470, MP 19) and that poses a challenge at every turn to the comfort of ignorance, this observation is both disconcerting and consistent—disconcerting in that it posits the inevitability of dealing with deficient knowledge, consistent in that it compels the reader not to ignore the problematical nature of knowledge.

By way of contrast to the telling epithets for knowledge, "superficial" and "imperfect," one can envisage an ideal of deep and complete knowledge, in the light of which man's cognitive acquisitions are inevitably relative. The categorical affirmations of the *Maximes* are not exempt from this relativity, which is the fundamental mode of critical activity. What is at first a criticism of an object becomes, in turn, an object of criticism, to be grasped in its partiality. In relation to La Rochefoucauld's lack of confidence in human understanding, the maxims take on, in the strictest sense, the status of fragments—of necessarily relative (and plural) truths, always already subject to skepticism, qualification, correction, or elaboration. The nominalistic character of the moralist's analyses constantly bears witness to the fragmentation of his knowledge, perpetually disseminated in the endless possibilities of linguistic designations and combinations and, more disquietingly, suspended or clouded by the interpretive malleability of abstractions. In order to speak of order, coherence, or "truth" *in relation to* the *Maximes,* we must initially seek to uncover that logically primary awareness of limits and constraints, that set of conceptual assumptions, which governs the aphorist's venture into the formulation of knowledge, orienting from the outset La Rochefoucauld's approach to ethical and axiological problems. In short, we must ask how the moralist—in apparent equanimity and with evident stylistic verve—manages to coexist with the perplexing paradox of knowledge.

Although knowledge appears to be at least potentially a problem for La Rochefoucauld (whereas language, despite the transparent conceptual looseness of abstractions and the overtness of aphoristic word-play, does not),[3] knowledge of knowl-

3. Cf. Jonathan Culler's incisive discussion in "Paradox and the language of morals," *Modern Language Review,* January 1973, pp. 28–39.

edge does not seem to be a doubly troublesome dilemma. Indeed, as an object of reflection about which truths are formulated, knowledge is ordinarily as unproblematical as any other
in the *Maximes*. In dealing with man's quest for knowledge,
La Rochefoucauld turns, as is his irrepressible custom, to the
contaminative role of egotism in human activity: "Blindness is
the most dangerous effect of men's pride: pride nourishes and
increases blindness, and prevents us from knowing the remedies
which might alleviate our suffering and cure our faults" (MS
10); "There are various forms of curiosity: one, based on self-
interest, makes us want to learn what may be useful; another,
based on pride, comes from a desire to know what others don't"
(Max. 173; see also Max. 36, 267, 494, MP 25). In the search
for knowledge no more than elsewhere can there be any question of suppressing man's innately egotistic motivation; rather
it is a question of directing the search for knowledge toward
what will be useful and away from prideful concerns that get
in the way of practical wisdom. To the extent that the critique
of perception and knowledge coincides with the exposure of
self-love, it does not threaten the learning process with invalida-
tion, it simply replays the theme of caution against the excesses
of unconscious, unregulated egotism. Studied self-interest is
typically viewed by the moralist as a support for knowledge,
guaranteeing the acuity of an individual's perception and insight.

A more serious threat to epistemological cogency in La Rochefoucauld's writing derives from the disclosure of the roles that
external factors (nature, fortune, circumstance) and unconscious drives play in the exercise of perception. In the course of
manifesting their power, these independent forces pose an
ominous challenge to the autonomy of consciousness: "Nature,
it seems, has buried in our minds skill and talents of which we
are unaware; the passions alone are empowered to bring them
to light and thereby sometimes give us a clearer and more
comprehensive vision than ingenuity could ever do" (Max.
404; see also Max. 36); "Circumstances reveal us to others and
still more to ourselves" (Max. 345; see also Max. 323, 470);

"Strength and weakness of mind are misnomers; they are really nothing but the good or bad health of our bodily organs" (Max. 44). Such observations do not touch directly upon what takes place in the acquisition of knowledge; they focus on the stimuli or modalities that condition its occurrence. Without discrediting perceptions that are triggered, for example, by fortune or passion, La Rochefoucauld calls into question what might be viewed as a lack of mental initiative, a kind of facile submission to the concerns—and thus to the areas of knowledge—that environmental and corporal forces impose upon the average man: "Through inertia and by force of habit the mind concerns itself with what it finds easy and pleasant; this habit constantly sets limits to our knowledge. Nobody has ever made the effort to stretch his mind to the limit of its power" (Max. 482); "Often, simply in weakness, we find consolation for woes which reason is powerless to console" (Max. 325). Like other activities, the attainment of knowledge can qualify as praiseworthy only if it complements natural merit (intelligence) with force and will. The knowledge of the average man is permanently retarded by the inherent passivity or servility of his cognitive faculties, the exercise of which all too often reflects an abdication of intellectual values.

Alternately supported by the critique of egotism (an object of blame) and by a rudimentary determinism (grounds of exculpation), La Rochefoucauld's skeptical view of human perceptions and, in particular, his unwillingness to allow man's ordinarily naive assumptions about the nature and extent of understanding serve at the very least to impeach the comforts of conventional (stable, commonsensical, readily expressible) knowledge. Yet do the *Maximes* go so far as to achieve a debunking of the general concept *knowledge,* which in turn compromises the pretension to knowledge and understanding implicit in the moralist's formulation of his perceptions? Does La Rochefoucauld fall into the snares of Pyrrhonism?[4] Just as the

4. Cf. Corrado Rosso, *Virtù e critica delle virtù nei moralisti francesi* (Turin, 1964), pp. 24, 28, etc.

Maximes and *Réflexions* refrain from granting that knowledge can be fully adequate, that truth can be whole or definitive, they desist from the inverse proposition that the inevitably partiality of knowledge entails the predominance of error or disables radically the search for truth. The instability of perception and the inaccessibility of epistemological grounds, powerfully invoked in the celebrated portrait of self-love (MS 1), preclude either extreme—thus preparing the ground for an intermediate position.

A number of texts, in fact, tend to set intellectual pursuits on a middle ground and cast them in a cautiously favorable light. The definition of truth in "Du vrai" (Réfl. I) sharply divorces the notion from a quantitative sense of completeness, stressing the *quality* of various truths that makes them equal in truth.[5] Moreover, the possibility of achieving on one's own initiative a critical mastery of rational judgment is recognized: "The reasonable man is not the one who discovers reason by chance, but the one who recognizes, understands, and savors it" (Max. 105). In the terminal juxtaposition of three intellective verbs, "connaitre" must mean to know the nature of, while "discerner" and "gouter" bring into play the ability to set reason apart and to derive satisfaction from adhering to it. The reasonable man is he who can take measure of the operation of reason from a distance and treat his own rationality as the possibility of controlled, judicious reflection—as a faculty that supports the exercise of good taste and underlies a certain intellectual pleasure, but not necessarily as a principle of perfect understanding. In short, the reasonable view of reason is simply the view from which reason is confidently identified and appreciated. The circularity of such reasoning—from reason through pleasure back to reason—is typical of La Rochefoucauld and, as a figure of self-perception, inscribes the essential complicity of the *honnête homme*'s rationality and his insis-

---

5. On the interpretation of this reflection and the notion of truth in general, see Hans-Jost Frey, "La Rochefoucauld und die Wahrheit," *Schweizer Monatshefte,* XLVII (July 1967), 388–94.

tence on perspective. In bringing to bear upon the exercise of the cognitive faculties (reason, judgment, intelligence, and the like) the same vital awareness of a sphere of application or validity that informs La Rochefoucauld's approach to the problem of action, the *Maximes* are recognizing explicitly the inevitability of a perspectivism that countless texts, still to be placed in context, show implicitly. Perhaps the most general formulation of this necessity (which dovetails with the predominant requirement of proportionality in La Rochefoucauld's ethical discourse) occurs in this maxim, which represents good judgment as a function of perceptual distance: "Men and their affairs have to be seen in the right perspective: some must be seen close up to be properly judged, and others can never be so well appreciated as from a distance" (Max. 104; see also Max. 365, 377, 436, 458 and Réfl. I, III, X, XI, XIII, XVI). The cognitive activity of the moralist precludes reliance on the perception of a basic, indubitable truth or on the pursuit of an argumentative logic; the reasonable, attainable goal of *good judgment* is a variable, dependent upon position or focus. Thus the exposition of accessible, appropriate "truths" need not take the form of a progression; the proliferation of shifting viewpoints will suffice.

In discoursing upon the functions of intelligence and taste, and by manipulating the somewhat evasive distinctions between *esprit* and *jugement* or *goût*,[6] the *Réflexions* go much further than the *Maximes* toward expounding the conditions of good

6. The distinction between *jugement* and *esprit* presents a rather sticky, if relatively minor, conceptual problem. Maxime 97 offers an apparent demystification of *jugement:* "Men have been mistaken in believing that mind and judgment were two different things. Judgment is only the extent of the mind's penetration. . . ." On the other hand, Maxime 456 suggests an operative distinction implying a certain superiority of the faculty of judgment over the mind: "One can sometimes act foolish with the mind, but never with judgment" (cf. Max. 258 and note 3, p. 66, Jacques Truchet, ed., *Maximes* [Paris, 1967]). In the earlier version of Maxime 97 (Max. 107 of the first edition), it appears that the meaning of *jugement* is limited to truth perception— "judgment decides what things are"—whereas in Maximes 258 and 456, which date from the fourth edition, it seems reasonable to associate the term with value judgment.

judgment. To be sure, as in the characterization of the *honnête homme,* La Rochefoucauld is obliged to underscore the rarity of those individuals who instinctively possess unfailing good taste:

They display more taste than wit because their self-love and their temperament do not take precedence over their native intelligence; everything acts harmoniously in them, everything is of one accord. This harmony allows them to perceive things judiciously and represent them accurately; but, speaking generally, there are few people whose taste is firm and independent of the taste of others. . . . It is very rare, and almost impossible, to encounter that sort of good taste which is able to assign its value to every thing, which knows its full worth, and which deals equitably with everything; our knowledge is too limited, and this just distribution of qualities which make for good judgment is ordinarily maintained in matters which do not concern us directly. When we are involved, our taste no longer has this soundness which is so necessary, it is troubled by preoccupation, everything which relates to ourselves appears to us in another light. No one sees with the same eyes what concerns him and what does not; our taste is then directed by the inclinations of self-love and disposition, which provide us with new views, and subject us to an infinite number of changes and uncertainties. . . .

[Réfl. X, "Des goûts"]

This text neatly combines a set of perfectly predictable values: intellectual independence, control of self-love by natural intelligence, truth sustained by unity and harmony. The disqualification of the judge from cases in which he is implicated results directly from the breakdown of "this just distribution of qualities," from a magnification of self that forecloses the maintenance of proportion in the subject-object relationship. Coincident with the change in perspective that invalidates judgment, an integral rearrangement of the dynamics of perception occurs, withdrawing the individual's cognitive powers from the control of his intelligence, so that his restricted knowledge becomes an insurmountable handicap for which the qualities of taste can no longer compensate. Thus the achievement of good judgment provides still another realization, within a prescribed sphere, of a delicate imbalance giving cognitive and intentional faculties a modicum of priority over other influences that shape human activity. Moreover, it is principally in and through the studied exercise of discrimination and judgment that La Rochefoucauld envisages the possibility of attributing to man a conditioned freedom, resting upon the limited independence of the self-conscious mind, which "is resolutely attached to its thoughts because it is fully cognizant of their strength and their justification ['raison']" (Réfl. XVI, "De la différence des esprits").

Whereas knowledge is theoretically deficient because of its inevitable incompleteness, the faculties of perception are subject only to practical obstacles that can be overcome under certain conditions. The critique of perceptual errors can be construed as an attempt to specify these conditions. Beyond this critique, moreover, still another positive note—comparable to the accent on taste and judgment—is sounded. Notwithstanding La Rochefoucauld's propensity for belittling the mind by representing it as subservient to the body and the heart or by opposing its activity to the exercise of good judgment, both the *Maximes* and the *Réflexions* display a remarkable deference to the *lumières de l'esprit*, to the undeniable powers of *pénétration* and *discernement*. Réflexion XVI characterizes at least two types of mind— *le grand esprit* and *le bon esprit*—which are endowed with an astounding concentration of perceptual and ratiocinative mastery.[7] An intelligence of such magnitude could only be, in La Rochefoucauld's view, a product of nature—*les lumières naturelles*—and it is in this context, where intelligence is recognized as one of an individual's natural qualities to which he

---

7. The characterization of a *grand esprit* is a fitting example: "His penetration has no limits, he always acts evenly and with the same activity, he discerns distant objects as if they were present, he understands, he imagines the greatest things, sees and knows the smallest; his thoughts are elevated, expansive, just and intelligible; nothing escapes from his insight, which always leads him to discover the truth behind the obscurities which hide it from others." It should be noted that *le bel esprit* is also treated with considerable respect in this reflection.

should remain true, that the full significance of continual stress upon the motif of rarity comes to light. The ultimate distinction between the great man and the common man, encountered in the imposing truth of death, derives from the latter's relative lack of intelligence: "In the indifference to death shown by great men it is the love of glory which removes death from their sight, whereas common men are prevented from realizing the full extent of their plight by their lack of understanding, which leaves them free to think of something else" (Max. 504).

In dying nobly, the great man has lucidly accepted the wisdom of no longer contemplating directly what the common man has never clearly seen. Throughout this long reflection on the deceitfulness of scorn for death, La Rochefoucauld, writing in the first person, builds up a firm correlation between authenticity in confronting death and an accurate perception of it. To scorn death is to misconstrue it, to understand it is to fear it: "Every man capable of seeing death as it is finds that it is terrifying." To account rationally for the experience of death is to envisage the change of perspective that the approach of death occasions:

We delude ourselves in thinking that death will look the same close at hand as we thought it did at a distance, and that our emotions, which are nothing but weakness, will be strong enough to endure dispassionately the severest of all ordeals. And we misunderstand the effects of self-love if we believe that it can help us to disregard what must necessarily destroy it, and reason, in which we think we find so many resources, is too weak on this occasion to persuade us as we would wish.

This remarkable passage, in the final maxim of the definitive 1678 edition, articulates a unique encounter in La Rochefoucauld's writing: brutally confronting the conflicting explanatory principles—internal cause (self-love) and external cause (death)—which operate singly in the critique of knowledge and perception, it marks the threshold beyond which neither principle can continue to engender error, that is, to distort the perceptions of intelligent men. As death puts an end to the possibility of disguise, the same change of perspective that, in moving away from objectivity and implicating the ego, ordinarily invalidates perception now has the opposite effect of guaranteeing its validity. It is precisely because self-love, powerless in the face of destruction, can no longer intervene that the direct, unmitigated apprehension of a reality to be experienced momentarily becomes possible, and it is upon his understanding of this unbearably "pure" perception—unmistakable truth— that La Rochefoucauld bases his counsel to turn one's eyes away from imminent death and onto other objects. Instead of "weak rationalizations" (Max. 42), he recommends a series of "remedies"—"the glory of dying with courage, the hope of being missed, the desire to leave a fine reputation, the assurance of being set free from the torments of life and of no longer being dependent upon the whims of fortune"—within which the common denominator is nothing other than man's natural penchant toward self-love. Holding consistently to the practice of envisaging action in terms of the possible, La Rochefoucauld ultimately appears less concerned with accrediting the search for flawless perception than with understanding the resources and functions of perception so as to ply them to a reasonable, practicable search for satisfying truths, worthy of studied assent. The need for direction and restraint remains paramount: "The greatest shortcoming of a penetrating intellect is not failing to reach the goal, but going beyond it" (Max. 377). Evaluating the use of intelligence means applying once again the fundamental ethical criterion of concordance between intention and action, means and end (see Max. 159–163).

An encounter with ultimate truth, the confrontation of self-love and death is also an encounter with the unknown. The absolute Truth which is Death is also the *absolutely unknowable,* from which man's partial, finite perceptions of himself and his world derive their status as the *relatively knowable* truths of finite existence. In conceding the worthiness of that life—protecting egotism that nurtures a self-centered knowledge, insulated from the paralyzing Truth of Death—La Rochefoucauld mitigates the force of his reflections on the technical impossibility of perfecting knowledge. On the one hand, the ideal of pure perception is demystified. On the other hand, the impossibility of perfect knowledge constitutes the necessity of a practical epistemology, anchored in a workable (partial but reasonable) understanding of the tenuous knowledge that actually develops and functions in human experience. As opposed to stern insistence upon a maximum of objectivity, the willingness to accept the permanent insecurity of knowledge underlies a relatively unpretentious intellectual outlook that squares with the moralist's decision to expose the reality of appearances and develop a strategy for dealing with them. To stress the limits of knowledge and perception is not to invalidate the processes of acquiring and stating knowledge—and thus, by invalidating the understanding of knowledge that the *Maximes* and the *Réflexions* present, to reduce the moralist's writings to insignificance; it is rather to set the formulation of knowledge in a human context, to tie it to a limited sphere of validity and intelligibility in much the same way that the judgment of action is tied to a sphere of accountability.

All the more clearly then, the paradox of the maxim, which does not disappear in the reflection, lies in the supreme confidence with which it states a relative truth, in the stamp of certitude it confers upon the problematical. It is no accident that readers of the *Maximes* have often seized upon the formal stability of the maxim as a mode of compensation for cognitive instability, for the manifestly calculated tone, rhythm, and rhetorical structure play so decisive a role in determining the immediate context within which the maxim must be read that one cannot simply treat them as a function of the author's stylistic zeal. However the relationship of knowledge to its mode of communication is represented, it is clear that identifying the limitations of validity as a leitmotiv in La Rochefoucauld's thinking revives the sense of a divergence of form from content. Apprehending the *Maximes* as a whole situates the paradox of the maxim in the irreducible tension that prevails between the specific formal context and the general intellectual context. In order to appreciate the depth and significance of this paradox, it is necessary to examine closely the structure and textual properties of the maxim.

Formal Representations of the Maxim

The recourse to formal analysis brings us back to a central observation of chapter 1: to inquire into the significance of the maxim's formal properties is, in the first place, to confront the difficulty of arriving at an accurate, nontrivial description of the maxim as a linguistic entity. The broad outlines of the problem are simple enough—in the area of grammatical and rhetorical structure, the *Maximes* display an immense variety, whence the difficulty of achieving a structural characterization at a useful level of generality without an inordinate number of exceptions or qualifications. The predictable approach to this problem has taken the direction of a search for kinds or species of maxims, resulting in typologies that tend to stress stylistic or rhetorical techniques. In an inquiry into the formulation of the maxim, it seems pertinent to review the findings of these investigations.

In *L'Art de la rose,* Lanson set the stage for much of the later research on the style of the *Maximes* by identifying various procedures of syntactical construction in given maxims. What was, in Lanson, a relatively casual approach to the maxim, viewed as a compositional game, subsequently became a much more earnest, systematic attempt to represent the form of the maxim. In the analysis by Arthur-Hermann Fink, who displays a statistician's interest in the frequency of occurrence of stylistic phenomena, the enumeration of rhetorical procedures (parallelism, antithesis, juxtaposition of opposites, surprising *pointe*) is preceded by an intriguing exposition of the maxim's geometrical configuration.[8] Rather than the form of a circle, of which the

8. Fink, *Maxime und Fragment* (Munich, 1934), pp. 22–33.

fixed center provides too strong a sense of completion, repose, and "closedness," the maxim takes the form of an ellipse: "La Rochefoucauld's maxim shows through its roundness a thematic tension that is brought into view as a form only by the harmoniously distorted circle, the ellipse, with its two foci or radial points, with its middle-point drawn out into two centers of tension: one focal point is given and the reader readily senses approximately where the second is located: harmonious tension and harmonious resolution as well (yet even then there is tension)."[9] The ellipse in question here is not to be taken as a static, mathematical figure; it is rather a dynamic, astronomical curve, which can vary in syntax from binary through quaternary forms. In addition to conceiving this geometrical superstructure onto which the syntax of the maxim may be fitted, Fink ventures some less technical comments on meter (which is often trochaic), on nominal style and the special role of personifications, on the frequency of propositions that re-evaluate conventional concepts, and on the contribution of these various stylistic features to the maintenance of baroque tension in the work. His overall emphasis on the binary opposition of substantives has been picked up by most of the more recent analysts.

A more exhaustive technical approach to the art of the maxim is adopted by Sister Zeller, whose great merit is to have begun by confronting directly "the complexity and multiplicity of aspects" that she accuses Lanson and Fink of neglecting: "What they have discussed in some detail are the more obvious characteristics of La Rochefoucauld, but they have done so superficially, with no final reference to the 'why' such forms or features should be his choice."[10] Conforming to "the exigencies of modern stylistics," Sister Zeller constructs a far more detailed analysis of syntactical and rhythmical patterns than Fink has envisaged, and complements this study with a systematic ex-

9. Ibid., p. 23.
10. Sister Mary Francine Zeller, *New Aspects of Style in the Maxims of La Rochefoucauld* (Washington, D.C., 1954), p. 41. Zeller's intricate analyses of the *Maximes* are in Part II, ch. I–IV.

amination of imagery, word usage, and grammatical components, as well as the survey of themes mentioned in chapter 1.
The attempt to cover such a broad range of linguistic phenomena
results in a bewildering conglomeration of widely disparate
data, thereby raising a plethora of questions about the significance of language use and the priorities governing it. Viewed
in toto, the study tends almost fatally to reinforce the considerable difficulty of developing an economical account of "maxi-
matic" (Zeller's term) structure, the parameters of which
appear to defy an integral perception.

For Sister Zeller, however, it seems possible to resolve (or
reject) many of the questions raised in her analysis by assuming
that a noteworthy phenomenon reflects some kind of conscious
choice by the artist, an ordering designed either to enhance
the esthetic qualities of his prose or to create a correspondence
between linguistic features and subject matter. Her initial treatment of syntactical forms provides a typical case. After recording numerous examples of bilateral symmetry, bilateral asymmetry, trilateral symmetry, and trilateral asymmetry, she comes
to the heading of multilateralism: "An observation which, up
to this point, seemed sporadically an evident conclusion, can
now be stated by principle: In some of the longer maxims, the
presence of a multilateral arrangement of terms gives conclusive
proof that the rhythmical pattern afforded by binomialism and
trinomialism was *definitely willed* by La Rochefoucauld as his
primary concern." The dissection of shorter maxims produces
an analogous conclusion: "There are also many maxims composed of one syntactical sentence, which, even in their unity,
allow a division into two or three members, with the same
variation of rhythmical patterns as have [*sic*] already been illustrated. This additional evidence proves conclusively that rhythm
is the structural force of the maxims, much more than the
thought."[11]

11. For the two foregoing quotations, ibid., pp. 65, 73; for the two quotations in the following paragraph, ibid., pp. 89, 91.

On the other hand, the discernible patterns of melodic effects seem to reflect a fairly considerable influence of the thought:

At times La Rochefoucauld runs the gamut of vowels, rising either to the highest, or descending to the lowest in point of articulation. This graduation also creates a melody in keeping with the subject matter under consideration.

The greatest melodic effects, however, are produced by the systematic combinations of the clear and grave vowels, woven in with the rhythmic pattern in such a way that the sentiments and grave feelings, and strong emotions, which La Rochefoucauld experienced and tried to portray to his salon listeners, were thus mitigated and more insinuatingly implied.

Whatever the object under examination, Sister Zeller represents her observations as evidence of calculated stylization, variously directed toward greater subtlety (effects of mitigation and insinuation) or more forceful impact (effects of emphasis and focalization). At almost every level of analysis, she provides a reasonably convincing confirmation of the fundamental tendency toward binary (bilateral, binomial, and so forth) ordering that Fink had stressed and that remains the focal point in every stylistic study of La Rochefoucauld. It should also be noted, however, that the crucial manifestation of this tendency occurs at the level of the clause or proposition, that the relationship of other binomial units (parallels or oppositions of parts of speech, phrases, or other grammatical features) to the primary syntactical structure in a maxim of typical length remains ill defined and, in a strictly stylistic context, is probably indeterminate.

Having confronted, thanks to Sister Zeller's conscientious and wide-ranging research, the initial difficulty of drawing significant conclusions from the massive accumulation of linguistic data, the critic finds himself in the position of the experimenter who is obliged to draw the line between relevant and irrelevant avenues of inquiry and to make some a priori discriminations with respect to the type and scope of observa-

tions that he may use effectively. Most of the recent studies of
form and language in the *Maximes* reflect an effort to identify
in advance a level of analysis, or even some characteristic feature of style, which should lend itself to the development of
insights on the relationship of language and thought, form and
meaning. Simply by applying with more rigor Lanson's technique of identifying types of formulae in the *Maximes,* Truchet
and Kuentz provide a reasonably cogent idea of what to expect
in the maxim. Truchet refers to the items of his typology as
"modèles" or "tours," while Kuentz's heading, "un art de
variations," suggests a somewhat more comprehensive view. By
comparing their topologies (the outline in the Appendix allows
for a comparison of some noteworthy analyses), we can see that
Truchet comes closer to representing the actual verbal structures
of the *Maximes,* while Kuentz details the potential for structuring with which the writer works. Both recognize explicitly,
however, that their inventories merely indicate a set of components which form the basis for an almost infinite number of
possible combinations.

If, in each of the various schemes of formal analysis, the
typical patterns of combination draw special attention, it is because of the assumption that they correlate with the writer's
characteristic patterns of thought. In Barthes's construction of
a formalist definition of the maxim, concentration on this correlation is especially important because he emphasizes language
as a determining influence upon thought. By comparing Barthes's
analysis to those of Truchet and Kuentz (see item III of the
Appendix), we can sharpen our sense of the way in which the
search for particularly meaningful forms tends to restrict the
breadth of analysis and to encourage the identification of fundamental, privileged structures. Upon completing his avowedly
summarial typology, Truchet comments judiciously that La
Rochefoucauld's "predilection for some of these techniques,
and his way of combining them, are personal traits which
characterize the turn of his mind." Barthes is less circumspect.

Affirming that it is specifically in the relation of restrictive identity (*n'est que*) that "the verbal structure of the maxim and the mental structure of its author come together," he will base his analysis of content on the relationships established in maxims that employ the *n'est que* construction.[12]

Other analyses of formal features in La Rochefoucauld's writing tend to be less comprehensive and directly addressed to specific phenomena. Harold Pagliaro's study, for example, while it does offer a kind of inventory encompassing the entire book of *Maximes* (see Appendix, item IV), focuses upon the types of paradox. Because he is primarily concerned with the act of cognition experienced by the reader of a paradox, Pagliaro has little to say about the author's role, except to note that he seeks to shock the reader into glimpsing truths that commonplace perceptions fail to reach. It seems safe to infer, however, that the writer must have experienced the same cognitive processes that his work demands of the reader and that the polar paradox might be taken as a particularly characteristic turn of thought.

Still more specific in focus than the studies of Barthes and Pagliaro is Rosso's commentary on the modes and structures of compensation. The privileged phenomenon here is the balancing process that comes into focus in maxims introduced by the concessive *quelque . . . que*: "Whatever difference there may appear to be among people's fortunes, there is nonetheless a certain compensation of good and bad which equalizes them" (Max. 52; see also Max. 3, 12, 53, 232, 255, 412, 473, Réfl. I, among others).[13] In maxims of this form, the principal clause appears to counterbalance the opening subordinate clause and to recover a certain equilibrium on a thematic as well as a stylistic level. Other procedures, such as the use of attenuating adverbs (like *quelquefois* and *souvent*) and syntactical propor-

12. Truchet, introd., p. xlvii; Roland Barthes, ed., *Maximes et Réflexions* (Paris, 1961), introduction, pp. lxiv–lxv.

13. See Rosso, *Virtù*, pp. 29–32, and "Démarches et structures de compensation dans les *Maximes* de La Rochefoucauld," *Cahiers de l'Association internationale des études française*, 18 (March 1966), 113–124.

tion (Max. 67, 115, 252, 274, and others), also manifest a
concern for balancing. In a more general context, La Rochefoucauld's agility in designating the relationships between
opposites might be taken as a reflection of a dialectic of equilibration, grounded in an esthetic, as well as an intellectual,
allegiance to the ideals of order, harmony, and rationality.

Recognizing that the enactment of compensation can be
readily conceived in either ideological or stylistic terms, Rosso
insists as strongly as Barthes upon the coordination of structure
and thought, but without conceding the priority of form. Citing
an earlier version of Maxime 52 in which "ait" instead of
"paraisse" is used in the concessive clause and *proportion* instead of *compensation* in the main clause, he supposes that the
definitive text, by reducing the difference between fortunes
from existent to apparent and thus relaxing the degree of opposition between the two clauses, accentuates the motif of compensation. In this instance, "the agreement between the structure
and the process of compensation would not be more complete:
in the form of a structure of compensation the truth of compensation is affirmed." Rosso's conclusion accords a clearer prec-
edent to thought over style: "The style bears witness to the
dialectic which generates it. And this dialectic sets up its relationships between apparently irreducible contents (the Fortunes
in their immense variety) and moves in the direction of what
one might call the myth or the ideal of compensation, equality."[14] Thus it should be in the movement toward equality,
where the stylistic and reflective achievements echo each other,
that a merging of form and content takes place in the *Maximes*.

In the diverse formal analyses that we have cited, one common point stands out: the bipolar structure of the typical maxim.
Almost automatically, the analyst of the maxim begins by look-
ing for two poles, usually substantives, upon which the rest of
the text turns; he thus tends to envisage the structuring of the

14. Rosso, "Démarches et structures de compensation," p. 124.

maxim as the process of relating those two terms. Qualifying a particular type of maxim amounts to naming the relationship that it sets up between its two poles. It is here, in the process of designation, that a kind of dispersion sets in, but whatever the types of statements or relationships that are distinguished (definition, paradox, explanation, generalization, restrictive, equation, identity, comparison, proportion, compensation, inequality, antithesis, repetition, and so forth), there is an unmistakable tendency to bring out, in the analysis of sample maxims, an underlying movement toward equivalence and/or equilibrium. To arrive at a more precise understanding of this tendency, it seems appropriate to examine three prominent cases that occur with high frequency and display reasonably specific structural features: antithesis, paradox, and restrictive identity.

Since the distinction of opposites goes hand in hand with the observation of human diversity, we find a degree of antithesis in nearly all maxims: "The interest which blinds some people enlightens others" (Max. 40). Given the opposite poles of blindness and enlightenment, this maxim relates them by representing them as possible results of the operation of interest. Evenly balanced in an either/or relationship, the two theses tend to cancel each other out, precluding either straightforward condemnation or full approbation of interest and favoring a "balanced" perception of it. Of course this has to be recognized as an ideal case, ultimately less significant than those in which one term of the antithesis enjoys some kind of preponderance over the other. As the following examples suggest, the *Maximes* demonstrate amply the wide range of expressive potential that stems from varying the context of antithetical relationships: "One often does good in order to be able to do evil with impunity" (Max. 121); "It is easier to be wise for others than for oneself" (Max. 132); "We do not scorn all those who have vices; but we do scorn all those who have not a single virtue" (Max. 186). The first of these maxims, opposing doing good and doing harm, sets the former in the context of the intention to do the latter, that is, it effectively exposes the subordination of good to evil; the second, opposing wisdom for others and wisdom for oneself, uses the comparative degree to underscore the disparity between relatively disinterested advice and self-centered judgments; the third, opposing the possession of vice as well as virtue and the total lack of virtue, closes on a decisive note of denunciation that established a clear preference for the former. In each case, the maxim furnishes a conceptual context in which one of the opposites takes precedence over the other.

Examining systematically the semantic poles of these texts suggests that antithesis per se functions to magnify the differentiation of signs that Barthes associates with the genesis of meaning. Removed from the rhetorical context that sets their relationship in a formal equilibrium, the opposites in question—even when transitive, rather than substantive, in nature—remain fully disconnected. In providing for the association of opposite terms, the structuring process of the maxim controls the distance between them and allows them to be grasped together, *as an antithesis*. But the finished text, while it may reduce the distance between its two poles and mitigate the force of their opposition, hardly inaugurates a movement beyond the polar opposition that can be seriously termed dialectical. Even in the most prominent cases of compensation (to which Rosso loosely refers as a dialectic), when the confrontation of the concessive and principal clauses does indeed achieve a kind of equalization, it depends upon a stabilization of opposing forces (for example, the known by the unknown, in Maxime 3; dissimulation by discovery, in Maxime 12; good fortune by bad fortune, in Maxime 52); this consolidation of proportion precludes transcendence of the antithetical relationship. The maxim deposits its antithesis in a seemingly inviolable form. Its artistic perfection, grounded in the elegance of syntactical proportion, resists even the slightest modification; its finality halts in its inception any movement toward synthesis momentarily generated by the association of opposites.

Loosely defined, paradox encompasses a vast majority of the maxims and frequently overlaps with antithesis. By analyzing the various types of paradox that he distinguishes, Pagliaro develops the thesis that "the opposing ideas in the paradox of every aphorism say the same thing in one important sense."[15] In the antithetical form, this means that each of the parallel members can be derived from the other and thus implies the whole paradox. The "essential reversibility" of the paradox can also be detected in the forms of equation (metaphor) and comparison, both of which play upon the presence of "similitude in dissimilitude."[16] This phrase reflects, to be sure, the limited degree of equality or sameness that the paradox requires. Pagliaro cites this maxim (which might be qualified as a definition, metaphor, explanation, reduction, or the like) in describing the function of paradox in the aphorism: "Most virtuous women are hidden treasures who are safe only because no one is seeking after them" (Max. 368). The image of hidden treasures clearly brings together the coordinates of the paradox, feminine virtue and the absence of temptation, establishing an identity between two terms that would ordinarily be perceived in terms of their difference. What looks like a contradiction on the surface, is more fundamentally a rejection of an out-and-out opposition; the contradiction is attenuated by a factor of resemblance (both the women and the treasures are protected from discovery) that underlies the paradox of undeserved value. In any paradoxical aphorism, whether the contradictory elements are stated or must be inferred, whether or not there is syntactical symmetry, its texture has a "unifying tension" that results from the presence of both resemblance and dissemblance in the relationship between its two parts. Pagliaro ends his argument by stressing the psychological aspect of reading the maxim, noting that, in the act of cognition, the reader experiences a sense of completion

15. Pagliaro, "Paradox in the Aphorisms of La Rochefoucauld and Some Representative English Followers," PMLA, LXXIX (March 1964) 46.
16. Ibid., pp. 48–49.

when he grasps the second polar element and passes from the level of commonplace perceptions to the deeper, enlarged understanding that the association of opposites opens to him. This sense of completion reinforces the finality of the maxim, contributing to the impression that a definitive, essential truth has been captured with the closing of the paradoxical circuit. Once again, the structure of the maxim represents the consolidation of a fixed, bipolar relationship.

The restrictive identity, as noted previously, has received considerable attention from Barthes, Starobinski, and other critics. Despite the obvious function of critical reduction to which the *n'est que* construction contributes, the relationship between the subject and predicate nominative remains a positive identity: "The clemency of princes is often only a policy for gaining popular affection" (Max. 15); "Love of justice is for most men only the fear of suffering injustice" (Max. 78). In these definitions, which link broad abstractions to narrower, egocentric motives, the equations (clemency = policy, love of justice = fear of injustice) suffice in themselves to achieve the demystifying effect. The adverbial *ne . . . que* does not signal a full-fledged negation, it is only a notation that makes explicit the exclusion of other substantive factors from the right-hand side of the equation, thus marking the completeness of the definition. The adverbial qualifiers adjacent to *ne . . . que* (*souvent, en la plupart des hommes*) underscore the limited scope of this completion, which confers upon the identification of subject and complement the same relational finality that pertains between the poles of antithesis and paradox. Indeed, these supplemental qualifiers, much more than the *ne . . . que* construction itself, acquire the status of negative factors in the equation, for they tend to counteract the restrictive element by allowing for exceptions.[17] In any case, the noun-copulative-noun axis that forms

17. Barthes's decision to treat restrictive identity as a privileged form is questionable on several counts. Almost any definition (identity) in the *Maximes* can be qualified as restrictive, and the *Maximes* achieve conceptual restriction in many other ways. Moreover, the definition is far less prom-

the superstructure of the maxim represents a relationship of maximum simplicity and equilibrium, even though the complete text, extended by the defining and explanatory functions of the predicate, almost inevitably lacks the symmetry between the two poles of the axis that we frequently observe in other forms. If, then, the restrictive identity appears, on the surface, to afford preponderance to the critical reduction of its subject articulated by the predicate, it ultimately constructs an "accurate" definition of that subject, which alleviates the sense of uncertainty that plagues the use of abstractions and, more directly than paradox (which reveals a single aspect of identity in a context of differentiation), validates the affirmation of sameness. Far from undermining the qualification of human conduct or attitudes, the restrictive identity, viewed in isolation, actually serves to place that qualification on more solid ground.[18]

It appears safe to postulate that fundamentally the equilibrium of maxims structured on antithesis, paradox, or identity rests upon the achievement of fixed relationships and a sense of finality. By no means does it follow that this conceptual stability necessarily entails a corresponding formal equilibrium grounded in an art of balancing grammatical or syntactical units. The structure of the *pointe* is an exemplary case, since it often involves a closing movement of the maxim which, although notably shorter than the first part, nonetheless exerts more than enough force to counterbalance it: "Philosophy triumphs easily over ills of the past and ills to come. But ills of the present triumph over it" (Max. 22); "We do not have the courage to make the general claim that we have no faults, and that our

inent in the second half of the work than in the first (one gets the impression that La Rochefoucauld exhausted the vein early on); and since the identity does not, for example, surpass the antithesis in frequency of occurrence or importance, one has to wonder if it is not privileged primarily because it leads in a certain critical direction.

18. The foregoing remarks on the basic relationships upon which the maxim is structured tend to support Barthes's conclusions on the non-dialectical character of La Rochefoucauld's vision. See Barthes, introduction, pp. lviii, lxxii–lxxv.

enemies have no good qualities at all; but in matters of detail we are not far from believing it" (Max. 397). As a rule the *pointe* is simply the second term of an unbalanced antithesis. As Barthes observes, it complements the ordinary language preceding it with an ending that calls attention to itself as a verbal spectacle while constituting the frame of reference that illuminates the entire maxim.[19] In its effect, the *pointe* is somewhat analogous to the closing movement of a definition, since the abrupt and forceful emergence of meaning fosters a strong sense of finality and certainty. In its structure, however, it remains tied to antithesis; pursuing Berthes's line of reasoning, one might suppose that the transparency of the meaning-generation process serves to reinforce the value and permanence of antithetical relationship. As a rhetorical device it illustrates the possibility of balancing opposites without recourse to syntactical proportion. Given the prevalence of syntactical imbalance in the *Maximes,* no more than a rough correlation between balanced syntax in a maxim and the conceptual equilibrium characteristic of its semantic structure seems allowable. An identifiable equilibration on the level of formal structure is unlikely to occur when, as in the definition, the underlying structure posits a relationship of equivalence. When, however, the basic semantic relationship in the maxim involves a process of differentiation, as in paradox and antithesis, some degree of formal equilibrium is likely to occur, whether achieved through syntactical symmetry or other rhetorical structures (including controlled imbalance, as in the *pointe,* and many concessives), and this equilibrium tends to reinforce the stability of the basic bipolar relationship.

Taken as an ensemble, the diverse studies of formal and stylistic features constitute a relatively loose characterization of the writing that the *Maximes* exemplify. The disparate results of these studies allow for little more than the obvious conclusion that the work incorporates many forms with much art. A

19. Introduction, pp. lix ff.

unitary global conception of the work—of its texture and language—remains to be formulated. While Barthes's structuralist reading is made more satisfying than most by its more systematic analysis and decisive orientation, his schematic representation of the maxim fails to provide a direct account of at least half the texts. In addition, treating the restrictive identity as a privileged form seems somewhat dubious in a work that strongly accentuates proportional relationships, advocating and illustrating the same harmony in language that it judges praiseworthy in life. In this perspective, Barthes's heavy emphasis on reduction and staticity may seem misplaced. Yet Barthes has clearly recognized the necessity (and demonstrated the value) of seeking out the elemental principles of sentential discourse, of grasping a certain dynamics that governs the elaboration of any maxim, of carrying out a reading of the *Maximes* that is commensurable with their fragmentary writing and with their status as abstractions, located on the periphery of literary language, closer to the rudiments of ideological assertion than to the refinements of style. Working toward these elemental principles of writing maxims leads to the realization that the analysis should be situated at a correspondingly elemental level—that the study of the maxim should be relocated on a less elevated plane than that of stylistics or rhetoric. In short, the analysis of those finished fragments called maxims ultimately leads back to the very basic perspectives of linguistics and grammar.

The Maxim as Abstract Discourse

A linguistic analysis of the *Maximes* proposes simply to define the maxim as a type of discourse, to pinpoint its distinctive traits. Serge Meleuc, whose article "Structure de la maxime" deals exclusively with the corpus of La Rochefoucauld's *Maximes,* emphasizes the high level of generality at which his study is conceived.[20] Since his aim—"to discern the formal constraints whose observance allows the production of discourse to take

20. In *Langages,* 13 (March 1969), pp. 66–99.

place"—has nothing to do with the particular message of La Rochefoucauld's book, most of his conclusions should be valid for any corpus of maxims.[21] According to Meleuc, two basic notions define the maxim as a type of discourse: it is the statement of a universal, and it is didactic. The requirements of universality and didacticism exert very strong constraints upon the composition of the maxim, "regulating, independently of the author, the specific form of the statement, sometimes down to the smallest of details."[22] In order to test this hypothesis, Meleuc undertakes two types of analysis. The first, "Grammaire de la proposition," entails a distributional analysis of articles, pronominals, and verb forms, plus a generative analysis of nominal transformations. In the main, the aspects of sentential grammar thus brought to light correspond to the constraints exerted by the requirement of universality. The second analysis, "Syntaxe interpropositionelle. La Transformation négative," is grounded in generative grammar; at the same time, it employs a communications model that specifies that, through the maxim, the author negates to some extent a "well-established" proposition attributable to the reader. In other words, the maxim carries out a negative transformation of the reader's proposition, thereby achieving its didactic effect. Thus, as an ensemble, the *Maximes* put into practice a rhetoric of negation.

Of the two aspects of this linguistic approach, the study of syntax, grounded in the specification of deep structures, provides the fundamental axis upon which the description of the maxim is based. (In this respect, the results of the generative analysis closely resemble those of Barthes's structural analysis.) Meleuc starts by dealing with a rather obvious case, maxims that report a statement and proceed to negate it. The force of the analysis lies primarily in the extent of the reduction achieved. Take, for example, this text: "The strength and the weakness of the mind are ill-named; for they are merely the good or bad

21. Ibid., p. 97.
22. Ibid., p. 70.

disposition of the bodily organs" (Max. 44). The negation of a reported statement (the mind makes the mind strong or weak) by a correction (the body makes the mind strong or weak) is readily evident. What is crucial here is the simple opposition of propositions (represented notationally as A vs. −A) to which the search for deep structures leads. The same binary opposition is obtained when much less obvious cases are analyzed. Meleuc examines two basic phenomena, "lexical inversion" and "syntactic inversion," which cover a very large portion of the *Maximes*. The results can be resumed by an observation that, since it is not, properly speaking, linguistic, is not formulated in Meleuc's study: either an antithesis is converted to an identity, or an identity is converted to an antithesis. In each case, analysis of the negative transformation shows that the surface structure ordinarily remains close to the binary articulation at the level of deep structure. The extreme simplicity of the latter confirms the notion that the form of the maxim confronts us with a maximum of coherence and semantic transparency.

The grammar of the maxim reflects a substantial reduction of the possibilities for building sentences that we observe in ordinary language. The use of verbs in the *Maximes* exemplifies this reduction. Not only is the verb *to be* manifestly preponderant in the collection, but the only significant opposition to be found in its verbal system is not an authentic temporal distinction (that is, present versus past tense), but an aspectual opposition of completed to incomplete action. As evidence that nominal transformations tend to suppress the verbal dimension in the *Maximes,* Meleuc cites the prominence of the infinitive. None of the verbal properties of tense, mode, number, aspect, or person can be attributed to the infinitive, which actually belongs to the class of nouns. Moreover, an examination of the forms *est, sont,* and *il y a* serves only to posit the semantic content of a statement, without indicating the temporal relationship between the stated fact and the discourse about that fact. Insofar as the verb of the maxim disallows the temporal and

personal modalities of expression, it links the text to the so-
called nominal sentence. Remarking upon the proverbial character of the nominal sentence, Benveniste connects the argumentative value of the verbally unmarked text to its location
outside the subjectivity of the speaker. In other words, the
didactic force of these texts stems from "the *nonvariability* of
the implied relationship between the linguistic statement and
the order of things." As opposed to narrative prose, the nominal
sentence constitutes the epitome of direct discourse. "Set apart
from tense, person, and circumstance, it is a truth set forth as
truth. This is why the nominal sentence is so well suited to
these statements, maxims or proverbs, to which, moreover, it
now tends to be confined, having once been a more flexible
form."[23]

In considering the implications of Meleuc's emphasis on
nominal transformations, we have to recognize that the prominence of purely assertive forms does not mean that the *Maximes*
forgo the semantic resources of the verb, that they are composed
solely of substantives linked by the forms of the verb *to be* (or
by other "weak" verbs, such as *to appear*). On the contrary, a
very substantial number of texts make use of transitive verbs, a
number of others use intransitives that convey action. Consequently, the verbal system does not, in itself, prove unequivocally
that the book of *Maximes,* like the dictionary, employs an essentially nominal discourse, stating definitions in the form of
universals. It is necessary to consider, especially in the case of
what we might call verbally activated maxims, whether proverbial discourse is strictly pro-verbal, whether it uniformly excludes the critical functions of personal and temporal reference.
Since, as Meleuc's analysis of deictic forms demonstrates, the
nouns of the collection refer to lexical items (that is, elements
of the semantic code) or to other elements of the statement in
which they appear, this question bears primarily upon the pro-

---

23. Emile Benveniste, *Problèmes de linguistique générale* (Paris, 1966),
pp. 160, 165.

nominal system. Among the forms of direct personal reference
(that is, pronouns in the first and second person, singular and
plural, which refer to interlocutors implied by the message),
only the first person plural is present. This, indeed, is the one
problematical case since the *nous* contrasts with the more common third-person forms *on* (or the class of all possible agents)
and *il* (or the class of inanimate and abstract referents) in two
significant respects: *nous* can encompass all of the personal
forms (*je, tu, on*); and if *nous* is taken to include addresser and
addressee in the field of personal reference, then it points to a
dialogic process of enunciation in the immediate present.

In this perspective, the simplest form of first-person statement
becomes the most complicated of maxims: "We make promises
in accord with our expectations, and we keep them in accord
with our fears" (Max. 38). Here, one can distinguish between
two temporal dimensions, the immediate present of the enunciatory process and the durative present of the stated universal, and
correlatively between two subjects, *we* who read or write this
statement and *we* who, as Men, act in accord with the principle
that is enunciated. The appearance of the enunciatory dimension
poses a problem previously encountered in the act of reading:
the distance between the reader and the text changes when the
reader is assimilated to the act of enunciation, when the observation becomes, in a sense, his own. As a problem of pronominal
reference, this change centers on the relationship of the statement to its origin, that is, it recenters the problem of reading on
the perception of the subject *we* (*nous*) and specifically on the
subject of enunciation, that is, on the identity of the personal
subject in the *Maximes*. Analytically, this subject clearly remains
inaccessible in texts like Maxime 38, which fail to distinguish it
from its impersonal and "suprapersonal" (*on*) counterparts. A
few texts, however, allow for an instructive differentiation:
"Hatred for *favorites* is nothing but love of favor. Vexation
over not possessing it is consoled and subdued by the scorn that
one shows for those who have it; and we refuse them our

esteem, not being able to take away from them what draws the esteem of everyone else" (Max. 55, italics added). As Meleuc observes, this text initially induces the reader to position himself with respect to the statement in which he is implicated, to adopt the stance of *nous* as opposed to that of others (*on, ils*). Nevertheless, the distinction of *on* from *nous* is far from decisive, for each of them serves as the subject of a proposition in which a pronominal substitute for *les favoris* (*ceux, leur*) is an objective complement. In other words, since *on* is to *ils* (they) as *nous* is to *ils, on* and *nous* appear to be interchangeable as subjects of a descriptive utterance, both designating the class of all possible agents. Thus it is only on the level of enunciation that *nous* can be differentiated from *on*. In the case under examination, the two propositions "l'on témoigne de ceux" and "nous leur refusons" fall within the same process of enunciation, that of the maxim, for the *nous* of the terminal clause clearly implements the articulation of the entire text. In short, a single collective subject governs the act of enunciation, just as a single subject of utterance underlies the propositions appended to *on* and *nous*.

Two kinds of consequences stem from the analysis of maxims that contain a mixture of pronominal forms. First, apprehending *on, nous,* and *il(s)* within the same process of enunciation allows the inference that all the maxims partake of this process, whether or not it is designated by the presence of *nous*. Thus the fundamental problem of the maxim (to which we shall return shortly) becomes more clearly the problem exposed by the first-person plural: how to represent more precisely the status and functioning of the collective subject of enunciation. Second, the referential parity of *on* and *nous* in the finished statement disallows the initial assumption that a wide gap separates maxims governed by *nous* from the rest of the corpus. In propositions in the first-person plural, a high proportion of verbs conveying action tends to reinforce their apparent divergence from the predominant nominal style of the collection. Yet they remain, contextually, closely aligned with the notional discourse of maxims built around the verb *to be*. In the text examined above (Max. 55), the combination of the opening definition and a longer proposition including *on* and *nous* corresponds to a juxtaposition, recurring throughout the *Maximes,* of definitional and illustrative statements. In relation to the general principle that is defined, the more specific observations concerning human experience take on the status of logical derivatives or verifying observations. In relation to the definitional vein of the *Maximes,* marked by the verbal mode of *being,* the observational or positional vein—of which the archetypical text is introduced by *il y a,* positing the *existence* of a phenomenon—plays a crucial supporting role, acting as a fully complementary discourse.

How, then, does this complementarity function? Here again Maxim 55 displays a characteristic relationship. Its movement describes a passage from an abstract notion (hate for the favored *is* love of favor) to concrete manifestations (one shows scorn, we deny homage), from idea to objective correlative, from the level of impersonal being to that of interpersonal existence, of feeling and doing. To support the encoding of definitive language is to affirm in parallel that phenomena conforming with the definitions *exist;* it is thus to anchor the discourse of being—of this copulative that is merely a mark of equivalence—in the perceptions of existence—of the verb *to be* in its strong sense, as a mark of reality. The articulation of a sentential proposition can ultimately be traced to one of two types of affirmation: x *est* (exists), or x *est* (equals) y. As one can see clearly in texts that begin by asserting the existence of a phenomenon, then proceed to define it (typically of the form *there is x which is y;* see Max. 69, 156, 173, 181, 193, 233, among others), their complementarity consists initially in the naming of the object to be apprehended (in a sense, renamed) in language, in its position within the semantic code. Even when the maxim incorporates a vivid development of the verbal dimension, sentential discourse remains profoundly nominal, is plied to a regimen of denomination that confers the mark of reality upon what is stated—that inscribes the word as a sign of existence or truth. From nominative to synonymal discourse, from the vein of the positional to that of the definitional maxim, we can trace the movement—always reversible—of nominalization. It is this movement that dissipates the full meaning of the verb *to be* by converting the affirmation of existence in time to a mark mediating equivalence or attribution in the space of language. It is also this movement that threatens to fix the maxim as an alienated discourse, abstracted from the immediacy of existence, displaying above all the relativity of its terms to one another. But by illustrating recurrently the convertibility of percepts to concepts—the possibility of nominalization exemplified by the transformation of *x exists* into *the existence of x*—the *Maximes* evince the dependency of definitional writing upon the fundamental act of naming, of capturing reality in language. In the texture of a work where "naming is everything," it is the force of denomination, carried over into renomination, that upholds the form of synonymy.

The dynamics of nominalization bear witness to a stylistic complexity that it is impossible to represent simply by emphasizing the preponderant role of abstract nouns. It is rather in a process of variation—in the shifting between the posing of a namable phenomenon and the juxtaposing of names, in the interplay of two relationships, one binding the sign to its referent, the other linking sign to sign—that the reader encounters the nominal discourse of the *Maximes*. Recognizing this variation is important if only because it precludes a facile condemnation of the work on the basis of its nominal—as opposed to verbal—*style*. The grounds of this opposition are well known. The tendency to replace subordinate clauses by prepositional phrases makes for more ponderous, congested propositions with fewer clauses per sentence; while making comprehension more difficult, this syntactic bulkiness results in a decrease in the number of basic sentence patterns, whence an increase in monotony. In addition, the heaviness of noun phrases and increased reliance on the copulative *to be* contribute to a sense of staticity, of scientific impersonality; they manifest the studied detachment of abstract writing from the engaging forms of everyday language. No doubt many texts in the *Maximes* exhibit the "defects" of nominal style, but as the verbal variety of the work suggests, the phenomenon is far from uniform or oppressive, and its expressive significance is hardly exhausted by the conative function. For nominal style is not a weak sister of verbal style, it simply fulfills another function and purveys its own order of meaning or mental activity. For descriptive purposes, Jakobson's celebrated distinction between the metaphoric and the metonymic poles can serve to illuminate this point.[24]

In its characteristic form, the language of the maxim is patently weighted toward the metaphoric pole. Indeed, it is difficult to imagine a discourse in which the predominance of associative relationships—here, terminological substitutions—is more transparently displayed. Viewed as a series of these substitutions, the *Maximes* focus our attention upon a paradigmatic dimension, the semantic field corresponding to a given socio-moral situation. Its particular texts seem designed to coordinate the components of the paradigm along their syntagmatic axis. Nominalization clearly goes hand in hand with this process of coordination. On the one hand, it serves to set the objects of reflection in a relationship of comparability, providing the elements of a conceptual system. On the other hand, by sapping the strength of the verbal dimension, it effectively limits the possibilities for syntagmatic development. In short, nominalization favors the subordination of the metonymic to the metaphoric, of combination to classification, of the principle of immanence to the principle of equivalence. Insofar as this metaphoric function superimposes the mode of resemblance onto the articulation along the syntagmatic axis, it disequilibrates the

24. Roman Jakobson, *Essais de linguistique générale* (Paris, 1963), ch. II.

complementary relationship of the two poles. The metonymic process of differentiating and contrasting elements within a syntagmatic whole is, so to speak, benumbed or modalized by the precedence of metaphor over diaphor. No less than lyric poetry, aphoristic discourse proceeds as if the space between words (or between the representations they relate) should be reduced, or as if the terms of speech should be pressed together in tighter relations that blur the distinctions among them and restore the opacity of signs, as if language should embody in its texture the inmixing and overlapping—the junctural magnetism—that overlay conceptual unity. In no sense, then, does the expressive economy of nominal style suppress the writer's power to densify and make ambiguous the frames of reference. In supporting the ascendancy of the metaphoric principle, nominalization necessarily supports the corollary emergence of equivocity, of the reflexive language of equivalence.

The foregoing glimpse into an aspect of sentential grammar brings out the presence, in the maxim, of what Jakobson defines as the poetic function of language: the "focus on the message for its own sake," which, "by promoting the palpability of signs, deepens the fundamental dichotomy of signs and objects."[25] Moreover, the specific definition of the poetic function seems remarkably well suited to the nominal and metaphoric orientation of sentential discourse, and seems, in fact, to designate a prominent structural feature of the maxim: "The poetic function projects the principle of equivalence from the axis of selection into the axis of combination."[26] While such a definition lends credence to Barthes's poetic notion of the maxim, it remains, as Jakobson recognizes, an inadequate basis for the analysis of poetic prose, located in a transitional zone between manifestly poetic and predominantly referential language. In addition to the referential function, the definitional

25. "Language and Poetics," in Essays on the Language of Literature, ed. Seymour Chatman and Samuel Levin (New York, 1967), p. 302.
26. Ibid.

vein of the maxim's discourse carries out a metalingual function (reference to the code—in this case, to the moralist's lexicon, to the system of relations among terms used in denoting aspects of human behavior). Jakobson presents the metalingual as diametrical opposite of the poetic function: "In metalanguage the sequence is used to build an equation, whereas in poetry the equation is used to build the sequence."[27] Now in the prose of the maxim, this diametrical opposition in the paradigm of expressive functionality is transformed into a symmetrical combination. The example of a straightforward definition, in which the metalingual function is manifest, illustrates this duality: "The refusal of praise is a desire to be praised twice over" (Max. 149). Poetically, the linking of "refus" to "désir" exposes "refus" in its role as a sign, consigning it to a suggestive wedlock that channels expansively its significative power. The invocation of desire confers on the refusal of praise a connotation that sets the sign apart from—as something more than—its denotative aspect, emancipates it from a merely referential function, and relocates it in the perspective of the message, in the play of the omnipresent metaphor of desire. At the same time, and also in contrast to the denotative or contextual function, the maxim makes a statement concerning the linguistic code: the refusal of praise refers to an instance of discourse—for example, "I refuse (your) praise," to be decoded as "I desire more praise." Within the code, what obtains is simply a relation of equivalence between *refuse* and *desire,* a pattern of sublimation through which the meaning of desire is modulated. Effective, creative communication depends upon the possibility of replacing *desire* by *refuse,* and vice versa, that is, upon the encoding and decoding of the metaphoric potential of language.

There is, then, a revealing coexistence of metalingual and poetic functions in the *Maximes.* When, in definitional assertions, the poetic function is paramount, its projection of the Word posits the existence of the metalingual dimension, dis-

27. Ibid., p. 303.

closing the spectacle of a connotative language that one cannot interpret except by adopting a discourse on language. In this sense, the *Maximes* combine literary and critical discourse; they both denote and illustrate the reality of connotation, they bear witness, directly and indirectly, to this movement through which language, in turning back upon itself, opens itself to the metalanguage of criticism. Running through the fabric of the work, there is, as it were, an episodic and primitive poetics (or at least an exposé of signs as signs), ascribing the vitality of meaning to the double-edged play of words against reality and against language. In the text of the *Maximes,* this implicit poetics of impository prose orients the perception of the enunciative act toward the dynamics of language itself, thus away from the representational language of the individual speaker. Or rather toward the play of language that submerges the subject in the process of nominal transformation and, in so doing, displaces the mode of personal expression with the discourse of language itself. Here again, a complex maxim combining personal and impersonal reference as well as positional and definitional discourse provides a valuable source of insight: "Constancy in love is a perpetual inconstancy, which means that our heart is drawn successively to all the qualities of the person whom we love . . ." (Max. 175). Reversing the movement of nominalization, this text reinforces the unification of the two propositions in a single enunciation. In linking very tightly, as if in a causal relationship, the assertion and the explanation of a paradoxical synonymy in the conceptual code, it excludes any separation of the subject *nous* from the addresser of the abstract principle. (Replacing either the articles of the latter by the possessive *notre* or the first-person markers of the subordinate clause by *le* and *on* would not change the meaning.) To specify the implications of the principle in agential terms is to determine the identity of the subject as a function of definitional discourse: the class of all possible agents (whether designated by *nous* or *on*) coincides with the class of all users of the code.

The maxim does not, strictly speaking, refer to a personal subject of enunciation, disconnected from the language it employs. The *nous* is the subject *of* language: as "the person who states the present instance of discourse containing the linguistic form *we*,"[28] it constitutes that *community* of users that grounds and guarantees the *communi*cative function of language. In other words, if we are to read the aphoristic statement in its integrity, without introducing a referential context (such as historical or biographical) suspended by the collection of maxims, we are compelled to grasp, in the collective subject of enunciation, the articulatory fulcrum of an abstract discourse in the process of constituting and validating itself. The extralinguistic referent of this *abstract* subject cannot be an individual author, the Duc de La Rochefoucauld, or the group composed by that author and his interlocutors or "fellow human beings"; within the rigor of the sentential statement, it is simply, and solely, the group of adherents to the lexical code inscribed in the text. This is to say that the *Maximes*, despite the apparent singularity of some of their ideas, present themselves as a fundamentally ideological—as opposed to individual—discourse.[29]

28. Here "we" is substituted for "I" in Benveniste's definition of the *Je*, in *Problèmes*, p. 252.

29. For a discussion of the ideological status of the sentential code, see Michel Pierssens, "Fonction et Champ de la maxime," *Sub-stance*, March 1971, pp. 1–9. In the following discussion, I take the term *ideology* to mean, in the first place, the logic of ideas insofar as they constitute a separate, self-contained system, as they are *abstracted* from historical and material conditions and seen to exist autonomously. In the second place, however, following the attack launched against the idealism of ideological discourse in the *German Ideology*, we recognize that independent, abstracted systems of thought are the ineluctable expressions of a historical situation which, initially and fundamentally, they serve to consolidate and that, in Marxian terms, ideological discourse is *representative* of the prevailing sociocultural order and of the dominant class. Given this rudimentary definition, it seems necessary to the dismiss confusing connotations sometimes attached to ideology, a term that has become something of a catch-all. In particular, the Marxian critique of German philosophy, leading to a theory of the absurd or illusory nature of ideology, engenders a pejorative use of the term, whereas I purport to use it descriptively. As for the extremely loose sense in which ideology is sometimes used to refer to any position-taking discourse (political, theoretical, etc.), this, of course, runs counter to the basic import of the

Between this ideological discourse and the rhetoric of negation, one might construe a certain contradiction, since the latter
systematically disrupts the dominion of received ideas. Indeed,
as has been often noted, the *Maximes* tend toward a certain
subversion of the prevailing ideological order, toward a reordering of social and ethical concepts that consists in reworking a
given semantic code. Now, the observation that rhetorical
patterns of negation mark the disconnection of the maxim from
conventional wisdom remains a vital step toward perceiving the
sense of constructing a substantial corpus of maxims. That step
must be supplemented, however, by a still more important one
that we can take in recognizing the functional priority of the
linguistic subject in the elaboration of ideological statements.
What must be understood clearly here is the relation of the
subject of enunciation to the subject of utterance. Even in abstract discourse, where situational factors and other indices per-
taining to the locutionary act are reduced to a near minimum,
this relation is subtle and by no means one of radical dissociation. Although the referential value of the collective subject in
the *Maximes* must be situated on the abstract level of ideological
discourse, it is nonetheless evident that this subject, as an object
of reference, is the target of critical negation or demystification.
The enunciating subject is at once coincident with and distinct
from that target; or, more precisely, the enunciating subject,
designated by the same pronominal form (*nous*) as the subject of the utterance, has no separate, independent existence.
Present in the act of enunciation and absent from the utterance,

---

concept in question here. Perhaps one further clarification is appropriate.
There would be much to say about the ideological thrust of La Rochefoucauld's writing with respect to its message or content: the key concept
here, and doubtless in the history of French moralist discourse from
Montaigne through the *philosophes,* is that of *interest.* But here we are
focusing on the form of ideological discourse, and in particular on the fact
that La Rochefoucauld's writing not only attains, but also maintains, a
very high level of abstraction (thus of conceptualization, idealization,
sublation, etc.), which approximates a "pure" state of ideological discourse,
in its detachment from personal and singular forms of locution.

it can only manifest itself through the act of referring to the very subject (present in the utterance, but absent from the enunciation) that it is not. Literary critics have repeatedly emphasized this dual function of the pronominal subject in studies of confessional and lyric writing, where problems of identity and self-consciousness arise within the gap between the "I" as an instance of discourse in the present and the "I" as a mark of selfhood implying the temporal continuum of the past. Whereas the possibility of accentuating and playing upon the role of the enunciating subject is a fundamental resource of first-person writing, it has limited potential in ideological discourse, primarily because the latter is articulated in a universal present or atemporal dimension, and also because the collective subject normally cannot stand apart from its past with the same decisiveness as the individual.[30]

Yet the thrust of ideological discourse does not have to be purely representative; it can reach beyond the expression of prevailing collective realities. It can be a critical discourse, one that prepares a shift away from anachronistic forms of representation or understanding, toward a transformation of the cultural codes and the forms of intelligibility that it unveils in their transparency—thus in their vulnerability to changing material and social realities. In order for this critical, transformative

30. It is indispensable to recognize the absence of a general analogy between the functioning of the first-person singular and the first-person plural, of the impossibility of attributing to the collective subject the kind of discursive identity—spreading into the whole psychological apparatus of self-consciousness, self-transformation, and so forth—that the singular subject can acquire through privileging the experiences of speaking and writing. In ideological discourse, the overdetermination of what we have termed the subject *of language* precludes this radical option and reminds us that analogies between reflexivity in language and the reflexivity of consciousness must be constructed with the greatest caution. The emergence of a metalanguage, as Jakobson shows in his celebrated discussion of aphasia, is a "natural" development in language-use and takes place *inside* the general topography of the language question, appropriating the terms and structures of the language to refer to the language in accord with all the rules and constraints that bind conventional language-use. This hardly allows us to envisage the metalingual function as the "self-consciousness" of language.

inflection to surface, it is necessary for the enunciating subject
to *appear:* the present instance of first-person-plural discourse
will serve as a mode of detachment from those representations
in which the subject of the utterance is entrenched. In the
Maximes, the occasional appearances of this plural subject of
enunciation thus assume a crucial role in determining the overall cast or tenor of the work. The Jakobsonian term shifter
seems remarkably appropriate here with respect to the deictic
form *nous.* Inscribed in the shift (articulated within the *nous*)
from the subject of the utterance to the subject of enunciation
is the arc of a discreet diacritical opening: a subtle assertion or
assumption of difference, distance, irony; the possibility of a
certain removal from the descriptive statement that is being
proffered, a certain distancing of the reality described through
the very practice of discourse itself. With this possibility comes
that of a certain effect upon—within—the subject itself, of a
certain adjustment or transformation, a mobilization, which the
separation of the enunciating subject from the subject of the
utterance elicits. It is precisely, and only, insofar as the collective subject of the *Maximes* is indeed able to assume the act of
enunciation and, through it, a split in its own identity, that the
book acquires a critical and subversive slant.

But let us insist again on the shift, or split, which is no more
than that, which is not a wholesale reversal and not a radical
disconnection. A decisive ideological break, one that unequivocally denounces a position of the past in order to set forth
another in its place, cannot be articulated in the space of a collective and universalist discourse. It requires instead an authorial
idiom in which the counterposition, while it may be speculatively
represented with a plural subject of utterance, can be only the
(less abstract) construct of a singular subject of enunciation.
The extreme rigor of La Rochefoucauld's writing rests on the
steadfast disallowance of this latter course, in the implacable
firmness with which it holds to the plural subject of abstract
representation, thus confining its work to the narrow space of a

strategic discursive shift—of a process of *shifting* within which the two subjects inscribed by the shifting *nous* are bound closely together, distinguishable only through a variation of perspective between referential and linguistic focuses. Moreover, the text does not display this variation explicitly or insistently. The effect of shifting is not to inaugurate the adoption of a new position (via assertion of the priority of the enunciating subject), but is merely to figure the possibility of making that move while reflecting, as well, the extreme difficulty of achieving more than a fleeting, momentary break—an ironic twist— with the predominant collective subject of the utterance. The latter, indeed, remains intact and unshaken, supported by the impeding language through which it is, nevertheless, in the act of enunciation, *exposed* and thereby placed in waiting, as it were, for a change that can be realized only through a change in language.

We have insisted on reading the texts of the *Maximes* in terms of the overbearing generality and the rigorously suprapersonal subject that sustain the extraordinary coherence of an otherwise disparate and disjunctive work. Against the background of this reading, Meleuc's strategy for explaining the work's effect through the opposition of the reader's belief to the author's correction no longer seems adequate. Insofar as the reader's experience consists in repeating the enunciative act inscribed in the text, his experience may also be one of duality, of a split identification. On the level of reference, the reader may be subsumed within the subject of utterance and thereby positioned as a "target" (thus subjected to correction). But on the level of discourse, the reader may assume the position of the subject of enunciation, of critical distance from the assertion that he is not making on his own, but repeating. In short, the experience of reading becomes, in its turn, one of shifting, and since the possibility of switching positions is ceaselessly regenerated throughout the work, the stance of the reading public is not fixed but remains ambivalent. In reality, of course, our

"ordinary" experience in reading La Rochefoucauld is still less
abstract and more complex, for we do not usually read solely
from our standpoint within a collectivity, and we cannot divorce
our reading from the dichotomy of the personal and the impersonal, of the individual and the ideological, with which the
Maximes confront us. The reader has to reckon with a plural
subject of language operating in a sphere upon the nature,
structure, and functioning of which an individual user of that
language has negligible influence, despite his ability to state
new meanings and express new experiences. In this relationship, the effect of distancing is pronounced. The difference
underlying it is the great and disconcerting difference between
the personhood operative in language and the everyday (psychological) notion of personality. This difference, in fact,
makes it somewhat hazardous to center an account of the reading experience on the protean notion of identification (even in
the modalized account in terms of positioning in language that
we have suggested above, the allusion to "split identification"
risks a metaphoric contamination by association with the per-
sonalistic term "split identity"). More important, this difference is what makes the reading of the *Maximes* a discovery of
language in its integrity and alterity, as the instrument that en-
codes and bespeaks us before we ever learn to play it, before we
discover in the play(ing) of language the secrets about ourselves
that it surrenders to articulation.

If there is indeed a certain sense of dual or split or shifting
identification on the part of the reader of the *Maximes* (an
identification that entails an association with or assimilation to
a discursive position, not a personal experience comparable to
the reader's attachment to a particular character in a narrative
or to a "self" expressed in poetry), there is also a reverse sense,
not of identifying, of stating oneself in reading the text, but of
being identified, of being spoken by the text. This opposition
of the reading subject's activity—the position of *subjectivity*—
to the action of discourse positioning the reader in language—

subjection—is, of course, the forceful and spectacular one that has so often been described, in diverse critical languages, by La Rochefoucauld's readers. Our point here is not simply to observe that it also contributes to making the reading experience an ambiguous one of continuous alternation between perspectives. It is still more instructive to note the extent to which that opposition mirrors the less obtrusive one of the subject of enunciation to the subject of utterance: it allows for a shifting of position within a relation in which the predominance of what is given in and by language remains paramount and defining for the subjects who are users of the language. In the reversal of perspectives for which the possibility of shifting allows, what we nonetheless discover once again is the limited potential, not for escaping from the forces of determination that weigh on us in every sphere of existence (in the present case, the force of overdetermination exerted by constituted language), but for a certain movement or opening within them, for a margin of adjustment, for a strategic skewing of combinations. In short, our inquiry into La Rochefoucauld's discursive practice discloses not so much a restatement as an illustration, at once delicate and powerful, of a sternly consistent assertion concerning man's limited potential for determining individual and collective action. However restricted in its effects, however modest in its pretensions, the calculated, *pointed* use of language is the *only* possibility for exerting a control over language apt to condition its evolution. La Rochefoucauld's writing states and assumes an imperative to seize upon that limited possibility, and it is precisely the rigorous application of that imperative which confers upon the *Maximes* their potent force of denunciation.

The characteristic discourse of the maxim—nominal, impersonal, ideological—is not composed of fragments, of parts broken off from a whole; it is rather a discourse of wholes, texts that are not just stylistically finished, but wholly abstracted, withdrawn from the verbal discourse of integration and from the personal modes of expression. We have argued that this discourse, insofar as it is confined to the processes of nominalization, of naming and renaming, is endowed with an almost inviolable coherence and conceptual rigor. Its consistency derives from the structure of a uniformative semantic code insulated from the continual fluctuations and *re*finements of individual language-use and is thus highly resistant to the possibilities for discursive development implemented in ordinary verbal communication. Consequently, the classical fragmentary writing epitomized by the *Maximes* is informed not so much by an impulse or discontinuity working to disestablish or disorient the rational framework of expression as by an insistent force of repetition sustaining the impression upon which logical expression is dependent. Perhaps the ultimate paradox presiding over sentential discourse is a function of the unfailing logic of repetition: abstract truth imposes itself in the *Maximes* in the ongoing process that parcels and restates it as a composite of truths; the singular force of knowledge is expressed by the persistent re-presentation of knowledge in its formal diversity. To write the abstract discourse of the *Maximes*—and to a lesser extent to write the normative discourse of the *Réflexions,* which often seems comparably abstract and disconnected—is to play upon this paradox at a level where it is most visible and revealing, where the variety and multiplicity of the moralist's statements do not hide, but actually underscore, their uniformity of import. For beyond the direct statement of man's limited potential for self-domination, La Rochefoucauld's language repeatedly marks the status of man as a designable, definable creature, comprehended by the language in which he comprehends himself, at once bounded and amply endowed, in his potential for understanding, by the medium in which knowledge is formulated. This recurrent paradox of cognitive discourse—grounded in the capacity of language to take measure of itself, in the inescapable coincidence of language and thought—embraces a relationship of unending fecundity precisely because, in its seemingly inhuman perfection, the discourse of the maxim represents the maximum of control that man can exercise over the language that defines him. To develop and refine the process of abstraction is to multiply and variegate the statement of our submersion in the cognitive field of linguistic structure and to defer, through the sustenance of difference in repetition, the closing of a truth that the paradoxical position of man within his language subjects to continual restatement. Thus the *Maximes* render suspect the conventional wisdom according to which the promulgation of abstractions is a dehumanizing activity reducing man to a helpless parody of the concrete, commonsensical creature who, in everyday life, takes charge of his destiny with minimal regard for the general principles that regulate it. To the extent that the relentless practice of abstraction achieves control over the dominant forms of language, to the extent that determined formulation of restraints affords a paradoxical detachment—if not liberation—from them, La Rochefoucauld's writing constitutes an immediate, self-validating testimony to the viability of the classical ethic of honesty that takes form in conjunction with it.

Appendix: Outline of Formal Analyses of the *Maximes*

I. Truchet (introd., pp. xlv–xlvii)
   A. General distinctions
      1. Rarity of precepts
      2. Abundance of definitions
         a. Subject/verb/predicate nominative
         b. *Ne . . . que*
         c. Combination of definitions
      3. Simple affirmations: turns and expressions for variations and nuances
         a. Qualifiers such as introductory phrases (*il semble que, on peut dire que*) or the insertion of *souvent, quelquefois*
         b. Expressions of universal scope: *on, nous, l'homme*
         c. Suggestion of vague quantitative judgments: *la plupart, certains*
         d. Categories of persons, designated by name (*les femmes, les jeunes gens, les vieillards*) or by relative clause (*ceux qui*)
   B. More complex constructions especially favored by La Rochefoucauld
      1. Paradoxes
         a. Rectification of a common error
         b. False suppositions

      c. Concessive clauses
      d. Proportions
      e. Inversion of subject and object
    2. Explanations

II. Kuentz (introd., pp. 32–33)
  A. Variation of terms
    1. Number
      a. Maxims with a single focus: often definitions
      b. Maxims with two foci: antitheses and comparisons
      c. Maxims with three or four foci: often syntactically aligned
    2. Nature: correlation of nouns, nouns and adjectives, adjectives, verbs
  B. Variation in extension
    1. Generalization: *on, nous, les hommes*
    2. Reduction of scope
      a. Examples
      b. Adverbial qualifiers
  C. Variation of relationships
    1. Equality: *être*
    2. Inequality: *plus que, quelque que, ne . . . que*
    3. Proportion
  D. Stylistic variations
    1. Figures of speech: simile, parallelism, antithesis
    2. Expressive techniques: repetition, paired phrases, trochaic meter

III. Barthes (introd., pp. xlvii–lxiv)
  A. Architectural foundation: predominance of substantive terms which are cornerstones, foci, *relata*, etc.
    1. Analysis: number of foci or strong terms
    2. Binary economy, classical symmetry
      a. Function of the odd term: mode of reference or relationship
      b. Complex meters (notably quaternary): metaphorical basis of compensation, proportion, etc.
  B. Centrality of equivalence: the sanctifying, poetic function of displaying essence (as opposed to *praxis*)

1. Comparisons: *plus, autant, moins* (function of denunciation)
2. Identity
3. Privileged status of the restrictive identity, based on *n'est que* (combination of disabusement and rationalization)

C. *La pointe*—esthetic intention
   1. Form of disjunction, often introduced by *et*
   2. Alternation: the privileged function of antithesis, which incarnates the genesis of meaning
   3. Repetition: the *pointe* as a verbal game

IV. Pagliaro ("Paradox . . . ," especially p. 45, note 11)
   A. Expository aphorisms
   B. Paradoxical aphorisms
      1. Polar
         a. Parallel structure
            i. Parallelism of antithesis
            ii. Parallelism of analysis
            iii. Parallelism of synthesis
         b. Equational structure
         c. Comparative structure
      2. Nonpolar

✤

Selected Bibliography

For this brief bibliography I have selected only those editions, books, and articles which contributed significantly to my understanding and appreciation of La Rochefoucauld. Much more extensive bibliographical information can be gleaned from the footnotes to the text.

EDITIONS

Oeuvres de La Rochefoucauld, Collection des Grands Ecrivains de la France, ed. D. L. Gilbert et al. 4 vols. Paris, 1868–1893.
Maximes et Réflexions, Le Club français du livre, ed. Roland Barthes. Paris, 1961.
Oeuvres complètes, Bibliothèque de la Pléiade, ed. Louis Martin-Chauffier, revised and augmented by Jean Marchand. Paris, 1964.
Maximes et Mémoires, Le Monde en 10/18, ed. Jean Starobinski. Paris, 1964.
Maximes, Les Petits Classiques Bordas, ed. Pierre Kuentz. Paris, 1966.
Maximes, ed. Jacques Truchet. Paris, 1967.
Réflexions ou sentences et maximes morales; Réflexions diverse, Textes littéraires français, ed. Dominique Secretan. Geneva, 1967.

CRITICISM

Adam, Antoine. *Histoire de la littérature français au XVIIe siècle,* IV. Paris, 1958.
Bénichou, Paul. *Morales du grand siècle.* Paris, 1948.

——. "L'Intention des *Maximes*," *L'Ecrivain et ses travaux*, pp. 3–37. Paris, 1967.

Coulet, Henri. "La Rochefoucauld ou la peur d'être dupe," *Hommage au Doyen Etienne Gros*, pp. 105–112. Aix-en-Provence, 1959.

Culler, Jonathan. "Paradox and the Language of Morals in La Rochefoucauld," *Modern Language Review*, 68 (January 1973), 28–39.

Fink, Arthur-Hermann. *Maxime und Fragment. Grenzmöglichkeiten einer Kunstform. Zur Morphologie des Aphorismus*. Munich, 1934.

Grubbs, H. A. *The Originality of La Rochefoucauld's Maxims*. Paris, 1929.

——. "La Genèse des 'Maximes' de La Rochefoucauld," *Revue d'histoire littéraire*, XXXIX (October-December 1932), 481–499, and XL (January-March, 1933), 14–37.

Hess, Gerhard. *Zur Entstehung der "Maximen" La Rochefoucaulds*. Cologne, 1957.

Hippeau, Louis. *Essai sur la morale de La Rochefoucauld*. Paris, 1967.

Jeanson, Francis. "Le Moraliste Grandeur Nature," *Lignes de départ*, pp. 71–107. Paris, 1963.

Krailsheimer, A. J. *Studies in Self-Interest from Descartes to La Bruyère*. Oxford, 1962.

Kruse, Margot. *Die Maxime in der Französischen Literatur*. Hamburg, 1960.

Meleuc, Serge. "Structure de la maxime," *Langages*, 13 (March 1969) 69–99.

Moore, W. G. "The World of La Rochefoucauld's *Maximes*," *French Studies*, VII (October 1953), 335–345.

——. "La Rochefoucauld: Une nouvelle anthropologie," *Revue des sciences humaines*, 72 (October 1953), 301–310.

——. "La Rochefoucauld's Masterpiece," *Linguistic and Literary Studies in Honor of Helmut A. Hatzfeld*, ed. Alessandro S. Crisafulli, pp. 263–268. Washington, D.C., 1964.

——. "La Rochefoucauld et le mystère de la vie," *Cahiers de l'Association internationale des études françaises*, 18 (March 1966), 105–111.

——. *La Rochefoucauld*. Oxford, 1969.

Mora, Edith. *François de La Rochefoucauld*. Paris, 1965.

Pagliaro, Harold E. "Paradox in the Aphorisms of La Rochefoucauld and Some Representative English Followers," *PMLA*, LXXIX (March 1964), 42–50.

Pierssens, Michel. "Fonction et champ de la maxime," *Sub-stance*, March 1971, pp. 1–9.

Rosso, Corrado. "Processo a La Rochefoucauld," *Critica Storica* (November-December 1963), pp. 638–653; (January-February 1964), pp. 27–48.

——. *Virtù e critica delle virtù nei moralisti francesi*. Turin, 1964.

——. "Démarches et structures de compensation dans les 'Maximes' de La Rochefoucauld," *Cahiers de l'Association internationale des études françaises*, 18 (March 1966), 113–124.

Rousset, Jean. "La Rochefoucauld contre le classicisme," *Archiv für das Studium der Neueren Sprachen*, 180 (1942), 107–112.

——. *La littérature de l'âge baroque en France*. Paris, 1965.

Starobinski, Jean. "Complexité de La Rochefoucauld," *Preuves*, 135 (May 1962), 33–40.

——. "La Rochefoucauld et les morales substitutives," *La Nouvelle Revue française*, 163–164 (July-August 1966), pp. 16–43, 211–229.

Sutcliffe, F. E. "The System of La Rochefoucauld," *Bulletin of the John Rylands Library*, XLIX (Autumn 1966), 233–245.

Zeller, M. F. *New Aspects of Style in the Maxims of La Rochefoucauld*. Washington, D.C., 1954.

Index of Quoted Texts

Index

La Rochefoucauld

Designed by R. E. Rosenbaum
Composed by York Composition Company, Inc.,
in 11 point Intertype Garamond, 2 points leaded,
with display lines in ATF Garamond.
Printed letterpress from type by York Composition Company
on Warren's Number 66 text, 50 pound basis.
Bound by John H. Dekker & Sons, Inc.
in Columbia book cloth
and stamped in All Purpose foil.

Library of Congress Cataloging in Publication Data
(For library cataloging purposes only)

Lewis, Philip E   1942–
    La Rochefoucauld.

    Bibliography: p.
    Includes index.
    1. La Rochefoucauld, François, duc de, 1613–1680—Criticism and
interpretation.   I. Title
PQ1815.L4   848′.4′02   76–28016
ISBN 0–8014–0848–2